P9-CRW-436

VISIONS OF
POWER

OF **POWER**

Ambition and Architecture from Ancient Times to the Present

by Adrian Tinniswood

STEWART, TABORI & CHANG
NEW YORK

For Emile Dietrich

VISIONS OF POWER
Ambition and Architecture from Ancient Times to the Present

First published in 1998 by Mitchell Beazley, an imprint of Reed Consumer Books Limited,
Michelin House, 81 Fulham Road, London SW3 6RB

Executive Editor	**Alison Starling**
Executive Art Editor	**Vivienne Brar**
Project Editor	**Elisabeth Faber**
Designer	**Lisa Tai**
Editorial Assistant	**Stephen Guise**
Picture Research	**Jo Walton**
Production	**Rachel Staveley**
Index	**Hilary Bird**

Published in 1998 and distributed by
Stewart, Tabori & Chang,
a division of U. S. Media Holdings, Inc.
115 West 18th Street, New York, NY 10011

Distributed in Canada by
General Publishing Ltd.
30 Lesmill Road
Don Mills, Ontario, Canada M3B 2T6

Library of Congress Cataloging-in-Publication Data

Tinniswood, Adrian.
    Visions of power: architecture and ambition from ancient times to the present /
by Adrian Tinniswood.
        p.   cm.
    Includes bibliographical references and index.
    ISBN 1-55670-650-2
    1. Architecture and state. I. Title.
    NA100.T56   1998
    720'.1'03—dc21   98-18774
                                                           CIP

Printed and bound in China
10 9 8 7 6 5 4 3 2 1

PREVIOUS PAGES **The glass pyramid at the Louvre Museum, designed by I. M. Pei as part of President François Mitterrand's architectural programme for Paris in the 1980s.**

CONTENTS

INTRODUCTION 6

CHAPTER 1

GODS, KINGS, AND EMPERORS 10

Akhenaten and the Horizon of the Sun-disc 14

Hadrian and the Pantheon 20

Justinian and Hagia Sophia 24

Suryavarman II and Angkor Wat 28

CHAPTER 2

HAIL THE CONQUERING HERO 34

William the Conqueror and the White Tower 38

Kubilai Khan and Beijing 42

Edward I and his Welsh Castles 46

Muhammad V and the Alhambra 50

Akbar and Fatehpur Sikri 56

CHAPTER 3

RENAISSANCE 60

The Medici and Florence 64

Francis I and Fontainebleau 70

Pope Julius III and the Villa Giulia 74

Philip II and the Escorial 78

Pope Sixtus V and Rome 82

CHAPTER 4

EAST AND WEST 86

Christian IV and Frederiksborg 90

Shah Jahan and the Taj Mahal 94

Toshihito and the Katsura Imperial Villa 100

Louis XIV and Versailles 104

CHAPTER 5

PALACES OF POWER 110

Catherine the Great and Tsarskoye Selo 114

Thomas Jefferson and Monticello 118

George Washington and the Federal City 122

George IV and Buckingham Palace 126

Ludwig II and Neuschwanstein 130

CHAPTER 6

THE GREAT DICTATORS 136

Peter the Great and St Petersburg 140

Napoleon III and Paris 144

Benito Mussolini and the EUR, Rome 148

Adolf Hitler and Berlin 152

Joseph Stalin and Moscow 156

CHAPTER 7

PRESTIGE IN A DEMOCRATIC AGE 162

The AT&T Building, New York 166

François Mitterrand and Paris 170

The Sultan of Brunei and the Istana Nurul Iman 174

Prince Charles and Poundbury 178

J. Paul Getty and the Getty Center 182

Bibliography 186

Index 188

Acknowledgments 192

Picture credits 192

The 1716 English translation of Palladio's *Quattro Libri dell'Architettura* has an intriguing frontispiece. Designed by the painter Sebastiano Ricci, it shows Father Time drawing aside a curtain to reveal a bust of Palladio. The architect is lit by beams cast by the Star of the Garter, like a saint receiving divine illumination from the Dove of the Holy Ghost. To the right Britannia hovers in the clouds, eyes averted, while two putti hold a royal coat of arms. On the ground the winged figure of Fame looks up imploringly at Britannia, as if begging her to draw inspiration from Palladio so that she can fly once more.

INTRODUCTION

RIGHT **Reflected glory: the frontispiece to Giacomo Leoni's English translation of Palladio links architecture with national prestige. The allegory is a striking piece of polemic, a call to George I to reaffirm British supremacy in the arts. By adopting an architectural style which has been sanctioned by tradition, it seems to say, the King can build a new, more enlightened future. Architecture is a weapon in a cultural armoury. Used judiciously, it can shower its patrons with honour, reputation and fame.**

OPPOSITE **An 18th-century view of the interior of St Peter's church in Rome, ostensibly an expression of God's grandeur, but in reality a very secular declaration of papal power.**

The power of architecture as an instrument of state policy was well known to those in early Georgian England, as it was to their immediate predecessors. "Architecture has its political Use, publick Buildings being the Ornament of a Country," wrote Christopher Wren in the 17th century. "It establishes a Nation, draws People and Commerce; makes the People love their native Country…" But Wren did not go far enough. Architecture does more than establish a nation. It establishes a ruler, a regime, an ideology.

Wherever we look in history, we can see this relationship between architecture and power at work – in the opulent buildings of the popes, created ostensibly for the greater glory of God and the Catholic Church, but more often as personal monuments; in the palaces of Moghul emperors and Russian tsars; in the cities of revolutionary republics and Fascist dictators. We can see it in the borrowing of architectural styles by the state for the sake of their associations, as a means of legitimizing a particular regime; it is a mark of the continuing power of classicism, for example, that statesmen as politically diverse as Thomas Jefferson and Joseph Stalin could turn it to their own ideological ends. The idea reaches a peak of absurdity in monuments such as Edwin Lutyens' War Memorial Arch in New Delhi (see p.8), in which a colonial power uses the architecture of a dead culture to express its dominance over a living one.

RIGHT **India Gate is Edwin Lutyens' memorial to Indian nationals who died in World War I. However, the form chosen – a triumphal arch – harks back to ancient Rome and carefully reinforces British cultural dominance in India.**

OPPOSITE **The Seagram Building in New York (by Ludwig Mies van der Rohe and Philip Johnson, 1954–8). The architecture of power still thrives in the later 20th century, although now it is corporate empires rather than kings who do the building.**

Intriguing though the political use of architecture is, we should not allow ourselves to forget that it has usually gone hand-in-hand with personal visions of power. In early societies, this perhaps meant little more than a warlord's residence being marked out from the houses of his subjects as bigger and more permanent. But there was usually more to it than that. Demons and winged, human-headed bulls decorated the entrance to the palace that the Assyrian King Sargon II built at Dur Sharrukin in northern Iraq. They gazed implacably down on those who took the long processional route through the palace to pay homage to the King. A relief at the foot of his throne portrayed Sargon in his chariot above the bodies of slain enemies, while his troops piled up pyramids of heads before him. Are the motives behind Sargon's eighth-century BC palace really so very different from those which gave rise to the interminable trek that visiting diplomats were forced to make through successive state-rooms of Hitler's Chancellery? "On the long walk from the entrance," said the Führer, "they'll get a taste of the power and grandeur of the German Reich."

Our own responses to the architectural excesses of past rulers are inevitably mixed. A sense of wonder at their beauty or grandeur is tinged with the uneasy feeling that in admiring them, we might unintentionally be buying into the values they represent. Perhaps we should simply focus on the architecture. Or perhaps we rest in the knowledge that such visions of power are most potent as reminders that power fades. Like Shelley's traveller from an antique land, we can survey the shattered remnants and smile ironically at the words on the pedestal: "My name is Ozymandias, king of kings: Look on my works, ye Mighty, and despair!"

CHAPTER 1

GODS, KINGS, AND EMPERORS

The period spanned by the four leaders who figure in this chapter is immense – almost two-and-a-half millennia. When the first of them, the god-king Akhenaten of Egypt, began to build his great city at Tell El-Amarna around 1350 BC, western Europe was still in the Bronze Age. Just a couple of generations before, the destruction of the palace of Knossos on Crete had heralded the end of Minoan culture. And of the most famous architectural landmarks of antiquity only the earliest was in existence, the Great Pyramid built for Cheops at Giza around 2600 BC, one of the Seven Wonders of the World. More than 1450 years passed before Emperor Hadrian began building the Pantheon in Rome; and another 400 or so before Justinian commissioned the Great Church at Constantinople.

PREVIOUS PAGE **A misty view of Angkor Wat, the temple-mountain built by Suryavarman II of Cambodia in the first half of the 12th century.**

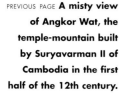

RIGHT **The Arch of Septimus Severus in the Roman Forum, erected in AD 203 to honour the tenth anniversary of the Emperor's accession. Beginning with Augustus, Roman emperors were routinely deified by the Senate after death.**

ABOVE **In 2600 BC, tens of thousands of workers were enlisted to move 2.6 million cubic metres (92 million cubic feet) of stone to create the Great Pyramid at Giza as a mausoleum for their Pharaoh, Cheops. The oldest of the legendary Seven Wonders of the World, it is the only one to survive today.**

By the time the most recent of these four leaders, the Khmer King Suryavarman II, built the temple-complex of Angkor Wat in the 12th century AD, Akhenaten's city had been deserted for two thousand years. The Roman Empire had come and gone, and its successor, the Byzantine Empire, was already in a state of decline. Like the civilizations that created them, most of the Seven Wonders had also flourished briefly and then fallen into dust. The Hanging Gardens of Babylon, the statue of Zeus at Olympia, the temple of Artemis at Ephesos, and the Colossus of Rhodes had all been destroyed; the Pharos at Alexandria was in ruins. Only the Mausoleum at Halicarnassus and the Great Pyramid of Giza still stood in anything like their original state.

Any attempt to draw parallels between cultures and architectures as widely separated by time and geography as those of ancient Egypt, second-century Rome, Byzantium in its heyday, and the Khmer Empire seems a dangerous exercise. Beyond the fact that Akhenaten, Hadrian, Justinian, and Suryavarman were absolute rulers and they all engaged in major architectural projects, they seem to have no more in common than the pure form of the Pantheon has with the stepped temple of Angkor Wat, or the open courts of the House of the Sun-disc with the ethereal dome of the Great Church.

Yet there is a common strand running through the architectural achievements of these four very different rulers. The purpose behind each of the buildings discussed on the following pages is religious; each was intended as a homage to a particular deity or deities. But the personal nature of the visions that created them meant that this primary function – to serve as a setting for the worship of gods – was overlaid with a more complex and secular symbolism, in which the builders not only basked in reflected glory by borrowing the odour of sanctity from their buildings, but in some sense subverted their purpose. The distinction between god and ruler was blurred, and their temples became shrines to their own self-regard.

AKHENATEN AND THE SUN-DISC

Akhenaten, the legendary heretic king who reigned over Egypt for just 17 years in the middle of the 14th century BC, is the most enigmatic and intriguing of all the pharaohs. He is famous for two things: the extraordinary way in which he tried to stamp out the vast pantheon of Egyptian gods and replace them with a single abstract deity, the Sun-disc; and the great new capital he built on the plains of Amarna and dedicated to the worship of the new religion.

ABOVE **Akhenaten attempted to replace the traditional Egyptian pantheon of gods with a single abstract deity symbolized by the sun. His name in fact means "Useful to the Sun-disc."**

OPPOSITE **The royal family worship the Sun-disc. The odd way in which Akhenaten is shown in contemporary portraits – long chin, tiny waist, and broad hips – continues to perplex scholars.**

Because of his advanced religious views, Akhenaten has seemed to many 20th-century commentators to be the very archetype of the romantic, doomed philosopher-king, a man born out of his time. The great Egyptologist Flinders Petrie, for example, who first excavated the Pharaoh's lost capital of Akhetaten ("the Horizon of the Sun-disc") in the 1890s, described him as "the most original thinker that ever lived in Egypt." For Petrie he was "one of the great idealists of the world." To Sigmund Freud, he was the man who showed Moses the way to Jewish monotheism. Others have been less charitable, dismissing him as an indolent dilettante who was content to philosophize while the Egyptian Empire fell to pieces around him.

The curiously expressionistic nature of contemporary depictions – full, fleshy lips, a strangely elongated jawline, an elongated upper body swelling into broad hips, large buttocks, and thick thighs – departs so dramatically from the usual idealized portraits of the pharaohs that some Egyptologists have been led to bizarre excursions into sexual pathology; at various times over the last century he has been described as asexual, transsexual, homosexual, a woman – even a visitor from another planet.

Akhenaten remains something of a mystery, although we can probably discount the idea that he was an extra-terrestrial. What we do know is that the King was born the second son of Amenophis III of Egypt, that his brother Tuthmosis died young, that he came to power as Amenophis IV (probably as co-regent during his father's lifetime), and that in the fifth year of his reign he changed his name from Amenophis ("Amun is satisfied") to Akhenaten ("Useful to the Sun-disc"). His father was one of the greatest builders in ancient Egypt, and during his time as pharaoh a series of mighty palaces and temples were erected at Memphis and in the neighbourhood of Thebes. True to his name, Amenophis III constructed or extended temples to Amun, king of all the gods, at Karnak and Luxor, built a huge palace-complex for himself and his wives at Malkata on the western shore of Thebes, and created a lavish mortuary temple with floors of silver, doorways of electrum (silver-and-gold alloy), and an entrance guarded by two statues of the king 21 metres (69 feet) high.

When Akhenaten came to power, much of this work was probably still in progress, and his earliest known building project is the decoration and completion of a gateway to his father's

temple of Amun at Karnak. But within a few years the young Pharaoh had grown dissatisfied with the traditional gods of Egypt and the Aten ("Sun-disc"), hitherto a relatively minor incarnation which co-existed alongside Amun, Osiris, and the rest, began to assume a new prominence in court theology. The King changed his name (an ideological statement as well as an expression of devotion to a particular deity), declared that the Aten was supreme among the gods (greater even than Amun himself), and for his first major architectural work built a new temple in East Karnak, which he called Gempaaten ("the Sun-disc is found in the house of the Sun-disc").

The Pharaoh's determination to place the Aten above Amun must have caused disquiet in court circles, particularly among the old Theban elite who derived much of their status from acting as priests to the king of the gods, and much of their income from the revenues that poured into Amun's temples. But while they may have felt uneasy at the way in which offerings which might have come to Amun were being diverted to the temple of the Sun-disc, they can hardly have expected what was to happen next. In the fifth

year of his reign Akhenaten declared that the Aten was not only supreme among the gods; he was the only god, and the Pharaoh his son was his representative on earth. The temples of Amun were closed down; their storehouses were emptied; and workmen were sent the length and breadth of Egypt to deface the name of Amun wherever it was found, on walls, in tombs, on artefacts and tablets.

Perhaps as a result of the hostility that these acts of sacrilege must have aroused, or perhaps as a final gesture of contempt for the king of the gods, Akhenaten also decided to desert Thebes, Amun's home. On the thirteenth day of the eighth month in the fifth year of his reign, he disembarked from his royal barge at a spot on the eastern bank of the Nile some 240 kilometres (150 miles) down river from the capital, a place where the sheer limestone cliffs that border the river curve back in a sweeping arc to form the flat plain of Amarna, about 20 kilometres (12½ miles) long by 4 kilometres (2½ miles) wide. In a state chariot of gold and silver he drove to where an altar had been set up for him to make offerings to the Aten. And as his assembled courtiers fell on

ABOVE **A fragment of a relief showing the Pharaoh and his Queen, Nefertiti, on the state barge. In the fifth year of his reign, he sailed down the Nile from Thebes to found his new capital, the Horizon of the Sun-disc.**

OPPOSITE **A fragment from another relief showing builders at work, and a cross-section of a house. Akhenaten declared in his announcement of the new city that "I shall build the Palace of the Pharaoh (Life, Health, Strength!). I shall build a palace for the Queen."**

their bellies and kissed the earth in his presence, he announced that the Aten had commanded him to build a new capital city – Akhetaten ("the Horizon of the Sun-disc"): "I shall build Akhetaten in this place for the Sun-disc, my Father... It belongs to the Sun-disc my Father [like] the mountains, the deserts, the fields, the isles, the upper lands and the lower lands, the water, the villages, the men, the animals, and all those things to which the Sun-disc my Father will give life eternally."

There was to be a new palace, he said, and government offices; apartments for the Pharaoh and his chief wife, Nefertiti; a House of Rejoicing; a House of the Aten, and a Temple of the Aten. A royal tomb was to be prepared in the hills to the east of the city, and no matter where he, his wife, and his daughter died, they were to be brought back to lie there. And all these works were to be done "for his Father the Aten, in Akhetaten, in this place." There was no room for any other god but Aten.

We do not know what the Pharaoh's courtiers thought of all this. Many of the officials who settled in the new city over the next couple of years seem to have been new men rather than mem-

"I shall build Akhetaten in this place for the Sun-disc, my Father... It belongs to the Sun-disc my Father [like] the mountains, the deserts, the fields, the isles, the upper lands and the lower lands, the water, the villages, the men, the animals, and all those things to which the Sun-disc my Father will give life eternally." AKHENATEN

bers of the old Theban aristocracy, who either were not invited or were not prepared to follow their heretic King into what they saw as a spiritual – and literal – wilderness. Perhaps more revealing of popular attitudes is the constant presence of the police and the military in depictions of Akhenaten, both in Thebes and later in Akhetaten itself. They are everywhere – marching, standing, bowing, but never far from their King and always ready to protect him.

The army was also put to use as an organized labour-force in building the new capital, which progressed rapidly. For the first year or so the Pharaoh, his wife (who was now called Nefer-Neferu-Aten, "the most beautiful of the beautiful is the Sun-disc"), and his daughters – "Beloved of the Sun-disc," "Protected by the Sun-disc," and "She who lives by the Sun-disc" – lived in a tent of

rushwork during their visits to the site. But by the seventh or eighth year of his reign Akhenaten was probably able to move into his private apartments, which stood on the eastern side of a north-south avenue. A bridge of mud-brick and wood linked them to the halls, gardens, and lodgings of the palace proper, which lay directly across the royal road. There were storehouses, workshops, and the mansions of courtiers, as well as more modest residential housing for workers and their families, and a settlement for the craftsmen working on the royal tombs in the foothills. To the north was the vast House of the Sun-disc, a mud-brick enclosure 760 metres (2494 feet) long and 290 metres (951 feet) wide, containing a series of open courts, the last of which housed a great altar. To either side there were 365 smaller altars, one for each day of the year, on which the King had placed the offerings of bread, meat, wine, and vegetables that fed not only the temple staff but also the city's population. Beyond this, at the end of an avenue of sphinxes, there was a further temple – the inner sanctuary of the god, where singers sang and musicians played while the Pharaoh and his family made their own offerings to the Aten before a quartzite stela and a massive seated statue of the King.

"Now His Majesty appeared as king at a time when the temples of gods and goddesses from Elephantine as far as the Delta marshes had fallen into ruin, and their shrines become dilapidated... This land had been struck by catastrophe; the gods had turned their backs on it. If the army was dispatched to the Levant to extend the borders of Egypt, they had no success. If one prayed to a god to ask something of him, he never would come at all... Their hearts were weakened in their bodies, for they had destroyed what had been made..." EDICT FROM TUTANKHAMUN

Scholars still debate the precise nature of Akhenaten's sun-worship. In the reliefs that survive from Akhetaten, Thebes, and elsewhere, he and his wife are typically depicted making offerings to the sun, whose rays terminate in hands bringing life and power (see p.15). The central tenet of the new religion seems to have been that, unlike the idols that lurked in the sanctuaries to other gods, the Aten was self-made, renewing himself each day and demonstrably giving life and light to the world. The famous Great Hymn that appears in the tombs of courtiers in the eastern hills of Akhetaten, and which is thought to have been composed by the King himself, talks of a mystical being who is remote, yet whose rays are upon the earth, who is within sight, yet whose ways are unknown. "The earth brightens when you arise in the eastern horizon and shine forth as Aten in the daytime... How manifold are your works! They are hidden from the sight of men, only God, like unto whom there is no other!" The temples at Akhetaten were open to the sky, so that worshippers could be in direct contact with the Aten, and to the south of the city there was a *maru* or viewing-temple, complete with pools, gardens, and open-air lodges, where the Pharaoh could commune with the sun and watch his progress through the sky. The impracticality of this notion in a country where temperatures can reach 40°C (110°F) was not lost on the King of Assyria, Ashuruballit I, who sent an angry letter to the Pharaoh after his emissaries had been kept standing in the sun at Akhetaten for such long periods that they were in peril of their lives.

The King of Assyria was not the only one to regard Akhenaten's new theology with suspicion and exasperation. After the latter's death, in about 1340, the brief reign of his son-in-law Smenkhkare was followed by that of the boy-king Tutankhaten, whose change of name to Tutankhamun suggests that the country was to return to the old ways. Foreign policy reverses in the Levant, plague, and

ABOVE **The interior of a courtier's tomb in the foothills to the east of Akhetaten. Never finished, it was built for the governor of the city, Neferkheperuher-sekheper, whose name means, in effect, that the pharaoh has created him.**

economic hardships were all blamed on Akhenaten's heresy, and in an official edict Tutankhamun declared that enough was enough: "Now His Majesty appeared as king at a time when the temples of gods and goddesses from Elephantine as far as the Delta marshes had fallen into ruin, and their shrines become dilapidated... This land had been struck by catastrophe; the gods had turned their backs on it. If the army was dispatched to the Levant to extend the borders of Egypt, they had no success. If one prayed to a god to ask something of him, he never would come at all... Their hearts were weakened in their bodies, for they had destroyed what had been made..."

The experiment was over. When Haremhab came to the throne around 1326 BC, conservative reaction set in with a vengeance. The temple of the Aten at Karnak was dismantled and its decorated blocks reused as infill for new buildings; the old capital of Memphis was reinstated as Egypt's chief city; figures of Akhenaten, Queen Nefertiti, and their children were defaced and their names obliterated; the image of the Aten was erased; and the Horizon of the Sun-disc was abandoned to squatters and looters. Like his vague, rather gentle religion, Akhenaten's great city, which had stood for scarcely two decades, disappeared back into the sand.

HADRIAN AND THE PANTHEON

The Emperor Trajan was consulting one day with Appollodoros, his architect and minister of works. They were busy discussing a point regarding the design of a new building in Rome when Hadrian, Trajan's young favourite and the man most likely to succeed him as emperor, chipped in eagerly with some thoughts of his own. He received short shrift from Appollodorus, who turned on him with the words, "Be off! You don't understand any of these matters!"

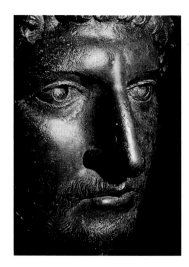

ABOVE **Although the Emperor Hadrian (AD 76–138) spent less than half of his 21-year reign in Rome, his keen personal interest in architecture transformed the city.**

Years later, after Trajan's death, Hadrian asked the architect for advice about his own designs for the Temple of Venus and Rome, the biggest in the city. Appollodorus was no less abrupt now that Hadrian was Emperor. The site was too low, he said; the design was wrong; and the statues that were intended to fill the temple were too big and out of proportion with the rest of the building. Hadrian pondered this advice. He remembered the slight he had received from the architect in Trajan's time. Then he had Appollodorus killed.

Perhaps this anecdote is no more than an attack on an unpopular emperor who died "hated by all." Yet it contains a germ of truth. Hadrian certainly did take a keen personal interest in architecture as an instrument of statecraft, commissioning an enormous number of buildings both in Rome itself and in the provinces. During his reign, which lasted from AD 117 to his death in 138, markets, monuments, and public baths were restored; the Roman brick-making industry was reorganized; at least three new temples were built in the city in addition to the Temple of Venus and Rome; the Emperor's great mausoleum that still dominates the skyline on the western bank of the Tiber at Castel Sant'Angelo was begun; and the 120-hectare (300-acre) official residence to the

north-east of the city, the Villa Adriana, where Hadrian devoted himself to art and debauchery, was completed.

To a certain extent, Hadrian was doing no more than following the example of his predecessors (notably Augustus, who reigned from 27 BC to AD 14), and working within an established tradition which equated the adornment of the empire with the power and benificence of the emperor. However, his interest in architecture was much more than that of a powerful patron. We don't know the names of the architects of the buildings erected in and around Rome during his reign – it is probable that the plain-speaking Appollodorus was one of them – but it seems likely that Hadrian was personally involved in the design of several, at least, in much the same way as an English gentleman of the 17th or 18th century might produce a rough scheme which would then be modified by a professional architect, surveyor, or mason.

Considering the architectural impact he had on Rome during his 21-year reign, Publius Aelius Hadrianus, to give him his full name, spent remarkably little time there. Born in southern Spain in AD 76, and proclaimed emperor on the death of his guardian Trajan, while Hadrian was Governor of Syria, in August 117, he did not turn

up in Rome until the following year. After a brief stay, he went off to Campania in the south of Italy and then embarked on the first of his "great journeys," a four- or five-year trek through France, Germany, Britain, Spain, Greece, and Sicily. He returned to Rome in 125 or 126, but after a brief tour of Italy and a trip to Africa, he set off once again in 128, this time heading east to Greece and on into Syria, Egypt, Judaea, and Crete, finally arriving back in the capital in 134.

There were sound political reasons for these prolonged absences: administrative reorganization in the provinces, the need to romanize outlying areas and placate restive chieftains, raising army morale, and so forth. Another more straightforward one is that at the beginning of his reign, at least, Hadrian would rather be anywhere but Rome – he did not like the ruling elite and they did not like him. As far as the senatorial class was concerned, he was capricious, offhand, and on occasion frankly contemptuous of their traditional rights and privileges. They in their turn felt insecure (particularly after Hadrian began his reign by killing four consuls for conspiring to dethrone him) and retaliated with snide remarks about his sybaritic lifestyle and his penchant for young boys. To be fair, he seems to have done his best to counter their hostility with kindness. His

ABOVE **The rotunda, 43.3 metres in diameter and 43.3 metres high (142 feet by 142 feet), is more than just a marvellous feat of engineering. The single ray of light that breaks through the oculus of the coffered dome gives the space an almost mystical significance.**

skilled free men. Politically, it helped to reassure the senatorial class that in spite of being an outsider, and a Spaniard to boot, Hadrian was aware of the importance of civic pride and eager to confirm Rome as the hub of the Empire. Personally, there is no doubt that the creation of so many new buildings was a form of entertainment; he enjoyed being involved in the act of artistic creation. And ideologically, it helped to establish the legitimacy of Rome's new *princeps*, or first citizen, by deliberately associating him with past emperors, particularly the great Augustus. It is no coincidence that the prototype for Hadrian's Mausoleum (see opposite) was that of Augustus; or that the entrance to his greatest architectural work, the Pantheon, was flanked by statues of Augustus and his son-in-law, Marcus Vipsanius Agrippa.

Begun within months of his arrival in Rome in 118 and completed within a year or two of his return after his first tour of empire in 125–6, the Pantheon replaced an earlier building put up by Agrippa at the end of the first century BC, which was then destroyed in a lightning strike in AD 110 – hence the confusing inscription over the entrance attributing the Pantheon to Agrippa (see p.21). This corroborates the statement of Hadrian's fourth-century biographer Aelius Spartianus that the Emperor "built public buildings in all places and without number, but he inscribed his own name on none of them except the Temple of his father Trajan."

The complex consisted of three elements. A colonnaded north-south forecourt with a triumphal arch in the centre led to a raised Corinthian portico, with 16 plain columns of red and grey granite and a pediment decorated with an imperial eagle within a wreath. Behind this portico, and linked to it by a rectangular block which rose 3 metres (10 feet) or so above the pediment and contained niches for the statues of Augustus and Agrippa, stood a rotunda of con-

sense of public responsibility was acute, even if it did not accord with theirs, and soon after he entered Rome for the first time as emperor, he wiped out debts to the state, burning the records publicly in Trajan's Forum. He also held a series of spectacular games calculated to endear himself to the population. And, most significantly of all for the purposes of this book, he began to build.

One can see a variety of motives present in his building programme. At a pragmatic level, it provided work for thousands of skilled and semi-

crete faced with brick and topped with a stepped dome. The brick facing may have been stuccoed; the first step of the dome was tiled with marble, while the rest was covered with gilded bronze. The long entrance court, together with the portico and the tall intermediate block, combined to conceal the rotunda from view, so that a citizen approaching the Pantheon in Hadrian's time would have been confronted by a fairly conventional facade – grand, certainly, but with scarcely a hint of what lay behind it.

And what lay behind it is one of the most famous architectural scenes in the world. The interior of the rotunda measures 43.3 metres (142 feet) in diameter and the same distance from the pavement of interlocking circles and squares in coloured marbles and granites, to the unglazed opening or oculus in the crown of the dome. The lower walls are punctuated with seven recesses, alternately curved and rectangular. In Hadrian's day they contained statues of the gods, while between them stood eight pedimented shrines or *aediculae*. The upper sections of the walls were decorated with coloured marble panels interspersed with bronze grilles which let light into the recesses.

Through the oculus a shaft of light ranges around the interior in a pattern which changes daily and seasonally, providing a metaphor for the world-conquering Roman Empire beneath the vault of heaven – and for the life-giving force of its first citizen, the emperor. The Pantheon was used not only as a temple, but also as an imperial audience hall where, according to his third-century biographer Dio Cassius, Hadrian "transacted with the aid of the Senate all the important and urgent business and held court." The conflation of religious and secular functions sought to place deities and state on an equal footing in the minds of Roman citizens. It affirmed that the rituals of government deserved the same respect as those of religion, that rendering unto Caesar the things

The Pantheon has attracted the admiration of generations of artists and writers. Michelangelo declared it to be "designed by an angel, not a man"; for Shelley, it was "the visible image of the universe." Stendhal said that it epitomized the sublime; Byron called it the "sanctuary and home of art and piety."

that were Caesar's and unto God the things that were God's was not an option in an all-embracing, all-powerful Roman Empire.

Though it has been battered and heavily restored, pillaged by Goths, and vandalized by popes, the Pantheon is still unforgettable, one of those rare pieces of architecture that actually meets the high expectations aroused by guidebook hyperbole. Hard though it is to strip away the overlay of 19th-century Romanticism and the aura of sanctity that stems from 1400 years of use as a Christian church, one still has a sense of Hadrian's Pantheon – partly a temple to the gods, partly an audience hall, and wholly an imperial and personal monument.

BELOW **The vast circular structure now known as Castel Sant'Angelo was built in the 130s by Hadrian as a mausoleum for himself and his family. It was much altered in the early Middle Ages, when ramparts were added and the tomb became the main fortress of Rome.**

JUSTINIAN AND HAGIA SOPHIA

Justinian, the ruler of the Byzantine Empire from 527 until 565, was the dominant figure of his age: a legislator who succeeded in codifying Roman law, a statesman who reasserted control over much of the old Roman Empire which his weaker predecessors had lost, a tireless advocate of religious orthodoxy who sought to unify a Church which was tearing itself apart – and the man responsible for Hagia Sophia at Constantinople, one of the greatest pieces of Christian architecture in the world.

ABOVE **Justinian (c.482–565) presents his Great Church to Christ and the Virgin, from a mosaic at Hagia Sophia. According to one of his closest advisors, the Emperor was "a moron."**

OPPOSITE **The interior of Hagia Sophia. The church was begun in 532 and dedicated in 537. At the dedication ceremony, Justinian declared "Solomon, I have outdone you!"**

The most striking contemporary image of Justinian that we have comes from Procopius of Caesarea, one of his senior government officials at Constantinople. According to Procopius, Justinian was "a moron."

The Secret History of Procopius is a devastating attack on Justinian, whom Procopius condemns as "deceitful, devious, false, hypocritical, two-faced, cruel," a faithless friend and a treacherous enemy, a tyrant who plundered countries, sacked cities, and enslaved whole nations "for no cause whatever." Chapters have headings such as "How Justinian Killed a Trillion People," "How He Spoiled the Beauty of the Cities and Plundered the Poor", and "Other Incidents Revealing Him as a Liar and a Hypocrite."

The censure extends to the Emperor's wife Theodora, an ex-actress with an uncertain past. Except that it was not all that uncertain, according to Procopius; he recalls with relish how as a young woman she regularly had sex with ten or more male dinner-guests before moving on to attendant slaves; and tells us that her favourite party trick was to lie on the floor while servants sprinkled her naked body with barley grains and specially trained geese nibbled them off again.

The Secret History was the result of Justinian's contempt for tradition, which aroused the wrath of many of the upper classes in the Byzantine Empire. This was not just reforming zeal, but a desire to outshine the past by breaking with it; and it found a perfect expression in his rebuilding of the "Great Church" at Constantinople.

In January 532 two rival groups of supporters at the chariot races, the Blues and the Greens, rioted when Justinian attempted to curb their street violence by hanging several members of both factions. Adopting their racecourse chant of "Nika" ("Win!"), they rampaged through the streets, killing police and officials, setting fire to buildings and laying siege to the Imperial Palace. It was only when Justinian's generals took mercenaries into the Hippodrome, where the rioters were gathered, and slaughtered thirty thousand of them, that the uprising came to an abrupt halt.

One of the casualties was the old Great Church, which was burned to the ground on the first night of the rising. Begun in the fourth

century AD by Constantine, the founder of the city and the first Christian emperor, the building's pedigree evoked the Byzantine empire's twin foundations in Christianity and Imperial Rome, and offered a concrete symbol of the emperor's God-given right to rule. As such, its reconstruction was obviously a priority, and work began on the rebuilding on 23 February 532, only 40 days after the fire, suggesting that plans must have been in hand already for a new basilica. Justinian had decided that the capital of empire needed a focus for Christian unity at a time when arguments over the nature of Christ's divinity were fragmenting the Church, and would confirm the Emperor's status as a new Solomon fulfilling God's decree that "He shall build me an house, and I will establish his throne for ever."

Justinian's architects, Anthemius of Tralles and Isidorus of Miletus, were both geometricians from Asia Minor. We do not know if they had any experience of building, although in any case, they were primarily theoreticians, relying on master-builders to make their ideas work. Those ideas were little short of revolutionary.

The church was approached from the Augusteion through a rectangular courtyard, colonnaded on three sides with a fountain in the centre. The fourth, eastern, side of this atrium formed a nine-bay outer porch or narthex. Beyond it, the main body of the building consisted of a central oval area aligned on an east-west axis, more than 75 metres (246 feet) long and with two galleried aisles to north and south. The eastern end was dominated by the marble ambo, or pulpit, which stood in the centre "as an island rises from the waves of the sea," according to the court poet Paul the Silentiary, who described Hagia Sophia ("Holy Wisdom") in 563. Further east stood an open chancel screen with its columns and parapets sheathed in silver, and behind this was the altar, covered with jewel-encrusted gold with silk and gold hangings, and standing beneath a silver canopy crowned with a silver orb and cross. The sanctuary alone apparently contained forty thousand pounds of silver.

At its consecration, less than six years after it was begun, Justinian's Great Church was one of the most lavishly decorated buildings in Constantinople. But the structural element that marked it out as the wonder of Byzantium was its enormous shallow dome, which floats like a

RIGHT **"And wondrous it is to see how the dome gradually rises wide below, and growing less as it reaches higher. It does not however spring upwards to a sharp point, but is like the firmament which rests on air, though the dome is fixed on the strong backs of arches."**

PAUL THE SILENTIARY, 563

BELOW **The church "is distinguished by indescribable beauty... being more magnificent than ordinary buildings, and much more elegant than those which are not of so just a proportion."**

PROCOPIUS, 561

canopy above the nave. Procopius, who produced an official account of the Emperor's architectural works as well as the definitely unofficial *Secret History*, wrote that "it does not appear to rest upon a solid foundation, but to cover the place beneath as though it were suspended from heaven by the fabled golden chain."

There were plenty of precedents for domed religious buildings, most notably Hadrian's Pantheon in Rome. But Hagia Sophia is an entirely different conception; while the Pantheon is a clearly defined circular space, the Great Church defies attempts to establish its boundaries, which advance and recede in a bewildering array of semi-domes, apses, and columned galleries so that the dome does indeed appear to float above them.

This is, of course, exactly the effect that Justinian intended. He took a keen interest in the progress of the building work, making regular site visits and even advising the masons on difficult technical issues. And while Hagia Sophia was certainly meant as a monument to God, His Church, and His Empire on earth, it was also a

The dome "does not appear to rest upon a solid foundation, but to cover the place beneath as though it were suspended from heaven by the fabled golden chain." PROCOPIUS OF CAESARIA

monument to the Emperor. His monogram and that of his wife Theodora adorned the walls, and around that altar there was an inscription beginning, "We [Justinian and Theodora] thy servants, O Christ, bring to thee of thine own..." – a reference to the episode in I Chronicles where King David, having made offerings in preparation for his son Solomon's building of the temple, says, "All things come of thee, and of thine own have we given thee."

The Great Church was dedicated on 27 December 537, with the Emperor in attendance. As the procession entered the nave, which was filled with the light from a thousand lamps, Justinian is said to have stopped short and gazed around him at the temple he had built. Then, in a gloriously inappropriate display of hubris, he exclaimed, "Solomon, I have outdone you!"

BELOW **Justinian's architects, Anthemius of Tralles and Isidorus of Miletus, were both geometricians rather than professional builders – a fact that helps to explain Hagia Sophia's purity of form, still evident after 14 centuries of change.**

SURYAVARMAN II AND **ANGKOR WAT**

Mention of Cambodia conjures up a kaleidoscope of images, none of them pleasant – carpet bombing and the killing fields, amputees and anti-personnel mines, child-soldiers with empty eyes, and pyramids of human skulls. Over the last 30 years the country has been devastated by foreign invasion and ideological conflict: six hundred thousand died when the Vietnam War spilled over into its territory in 1970; two million more died as a result of the Khmer Rouge's reign of terror from 1975 to 1978.

ABOVE **Part of a relief in the Outer Gallery at Angkor Wat, showing the temple's builder Suryavarman II, the 12th-century ruler of the Khmer Empire.**

OPPOSITE **The Sanctuary of Vishnu was housed in the central tower of the complex – a metaphor in elaborately ornamented stone for Mount Meru, the home of the gods in Hindu teachings.**

If it makes any sense at all to describe a country as "unhappy," then Cambodia deserves that epithet more than most. However, such dreadful images of suffering and destruction make it easy to forget that a thousand years ago, while most of western Europe was still struggling to emerge from the Dark Ages, Cambodia was already a powerful and sophisticated empire, one of the most significant forces in south-east Asia. The wooden palaces of its kings have long since disappeared, but the temple-mountains, which they built to define their right to rule and to proclaim their relationship with the gods, still survive. A number of these startling monuments can still be seen at Angkor, the royal city of the ancient Khmer Empire, which lies about 300 kilometres (186 miles) north-west of the present-day capital of Phnom Penh. And the greatest and most famous of the Angkorean temples is Angkor Wat, the temple-mountain built by Suryavarman II in the first half of the 12th century.

As with most of the early Cambodian kings, little is known for certain about Suryavarman II. Possibly the nephew of his predecessor, Jayavarman VI, he came to power in the 1110s or 1120s by defeating a rival claimant, after a long period during which the kingdom had suffered from particularly vicious factional in-fighting. A contemporary inscription states that "leaving the ocean of his army on the field of combat... he bounded to the head of the elephant of the enemy king, and killed him as a *garuda* [a mythical bird with a human body] on the slope of a mountain might kill a snake." Between his accession to the throne and his death in about 1150, he pursued a vigorous and pragmatic foreign policy; besides unifying the country for the first time in 50 years, he established useful diplomatic and trading links with China, and forged an alliance with Cambodia's traditional enemies, the Chams who lived to the east, to make war on their other traditional enemies, the Vietnamese.

Like so many rulers before and since, Suryavarman also moved quickly to establish his reign as separate from and superior to those that had gone before. One of the most public ways to do this in Khmer society was through the adoption of a particular patron-deity, and the usual

"Leaving the ocean of his army on the field of combat... he bounded to the head of the elephant of the enemy king, and killed him as a *garuda* [a mythical bird with a human body] on the slope of a mountain might kill a snake." CONTEMPORARY INSCRIPTION

architectural expression of this special relationship was the temple-mountain which housed the image of the chosen patron. A number of these survive in and around Angkor, together with their great reservoirs and moats, ritual evocations of the waters which surrounded Mount Meru, the legendary home of the gods to the north of the Himalayas, which was thought to be at the exact centre of the world.

The Cambodians were quite easy-going about religious matters. Ancestor-worship, Hinduism, and various varieties of Buddhism co-existed on amicable terms, and occasionally blended together in what to Western eyes is a rather bewildering melange. For example, Yasovarman I (reigned 889–c.910), who established the royal capital at Angkor (then known as Yasodharapura), was a Hindu; however, he built a series of monasteries for both Hindu and Buddhist monks, as well as erecting four temples in honour of his parents. Jayavarman IV, who came to the throne in 928, was a follower of the Hindu deity Siva, the Destroyer and also, since death brings life, the Creator; Jayavarman was also one of the first Cambodian kings to draw his authority from the fact that he was in some sense part of the god, who was housed in his temple-mountain and to whom he would return at his death – a notion adopted by his successors, including Suryavarman II, even if they differed as to exactly which god it was. Other kings were converts to Buddhism.

BELOW **A group of *apsaras*, celestial dancing girls. The 800 metres (2625 feet) of sandstone carvings that decorate the Outer Gallery are said to form the longest bas-relief in the world.**

Suryavarman was the first Khmer king to name Vishnu as his patron-deity, and Angkor Wat was the only temple-mountain at Angkor to be dedicated to the god. In traditional Vedic teachings, Vishnu the Protector of the World is part of the trinity that rules the whole universe, together with Brahma the Creator and Siva the Destroyer. He has many incarnations, although not all were to be found in Khmer Cambodia; Krishna and Rama, the heroes of the epics *Ramayana* and *Mahabharata*, were the most common, and both appear at Angkor Wat. Vishnu was originally a deification of the sun, and Suryavarman's name, which means "protected by the sun," may well be a reflection of his one-ness with Vishnu. When Suryavarman II came to power, Angkor Thom (literally, "large town") had been the capital of the Khmer Empire on and off for some two hundred years, and successive kings had made their mark there in the usual way, by building temple-mountains and creating great reservoirs and lakes. There are still two schools of thought about these artificial lakes, which were often of immense size, measuring up to 8 kilometres (5 miles) in length; one theory holds that they were primarily used to irrigate the surrounding ricefields, the other that they were of purely ritual significance as symbols of the waters that surrounded Mount Meru. The kings also erected residential palaces and administrative blocks, but no traces of these survive, presumably because they were built of wood, in contrast to the more durable laterite and sandstone that were used for the temples.

The site that Suryavarman chose for his own temple-mountain was in the south-east corner of Yasovarman's capital, in an area relatively free of permanent buildings. A rectangular moat 200 metres (656 feet) across encloses a level platform 1.5 kilometres by 1.3 kilometres (0.9 miles by 0.8 miles) aligned on the cardinal points of the compass, with its long axis running from west to east.

In contrast to the usual Khmer practice of placing the entrance to a temple on the eastern side, access to the complex is from the west, via a processional causeway that runs through a triple-towered gateway and on, past two pavilions (usually called "libraries") and two rectangular pools, to a walled enclosure, where the sacred area of the temple finally begins with a cross-shaped court or cloister where ritual dances may have been performed.

A Khmer temple was the home of a god rather than a place of assembly for the faithful, and there is no prayer hall where a congregation could gather at Angkor Wat. It is basically a shrine conceived on a colossal scale, consisting of three rectangular terraces diminishing in size to form

the stepped pyramid that was meant to evoke Mount Meru. The third and highest terrace is flanked by four conical towers, with a fifth, which rises 42 metres (138 feet) above the terrace, at their centre. This highest turret, the summit of the "mountain," marks the sanctuary where Vishnu lived.

The lowest and largest terrace, which measures 215 metres by 187 metres (705 feet by 614 feet), is enclosed within an open and partly vaulted gallery, the four inner walls of which are completely covered with intricate sandstone carvings (see opposite). In a series of huge and breathtakingly beautiful panels, it depicts stories from the Ramayana and the Mahabharata and scenes from Suryavarman II's reign. Enthroned

ABOVE **The processional route from the entrance to the central tower (shown here) is part of an allegory in which one travels backwards through the Four Ages of Indian cosmology, finally reaching the sanctuary and the first, Golden Age. Only Suryavarman and his high priest would have been permitted to penetrate that far.**

The best way for an invader to maintain dominance over a conquered people, without constantly having to resort to expensive and destabilizing military force, is to impose its own cultural values and priorities. This might come about in various ways: by discouraging or prohibiting native arts; by suppressing native languages, as European settlers did in America and the English tried to do in Scotland, Wales and Ireland; by ensuring that government business is carried on in the invader's language even when that business is delegated to natives, as the Normans did in England and the British did throughout their Empire; and, of course, by dismantling public buildings and replacing them with others in an architectural style that confirms the supremacy of the new regime.

PREVIOUS PAGE **The Tropaeum Alpinum at La Turbie in the hills above Monte Carlo, which commemorates the victory of Augustus' imperial legions over 44 Alpine tribes in the area.**

RIGHT **Roman remains at Timgad in Algeria. An outpost on the edge of empire, Timgad boasted a basilica, a forum, and 11 public baths, all of which encouraged its inhabitants both to buy into the benefits of Roman civilization, and to understand where their allegiances should lie.**

LEFT **The Spanish baroque facade of the 16th-century church of Santo Domingo in San Christobal, Mexico. Imposing alien architectural forms on a vanquished race has always been an integral part of conquest.**

OPPOSITE **F. W. Stevens' Victoria Railway Terminus in Bombay was begun in 1877 and named for the Queen Empress on Jubilee Day, 1887. Although its Indo-Gothic design pays lip service to local tradition, western European architectural forms remain firmly in control.**

western European architectural idioms. The bombs dropped on Ethiopia during Mussolini's annexation in the 1930s were followed by monumentalist buildings that bludgeoned the local culture into submission – less violently, but no less harshly.

The building enterprises that feature in this chapter represent diverse responses to military victory. The castles of William I and Edward I are essentially utilitarian power-bases for ruling elites in hostile societies. The Alhambra is more properly described as a retrenchment than a conquest, an attempt by the sultans of Granada to hold on to power; while Akbar's "City of Victory" is as unhinged as its builder in its mystical vision of a new religion that would unify the disparate peoples of Moghul India. Ironically, given his reputation as a barbarian, Kubilai Khan's palace at Beijing shows the most sophisticated response of the five. He alone had the sense to take the indigenous architecture, to turn it around, and to offer it back to a vanquished people as his own creation. Now that really is a victory.

The Romans were the experts. Citizens of the Empire travelling along the coast from Italy to southern France, for example, would be reassured by the sight of the monumental Tropaeum Alpinum at La Turbie in the hills above Monte Carlo (see pp.34–5), which records the names of the 44 Alpine tribes in the area subdued by Augustus. Those who lived in Algeria and Libya could wander round the forum at Timgad or enjoy the races in the Circus at Leptis Magna; in Portugal, they could relax in the public baths of Conimbriga, while in Britannia they might trade in the basilica at Silchester. On the eastern frontiers, they could practise the state religion in temples at Palmyra, or Ba'albek in the Lebanese hills. Such buildings defined empire, helping to bring together diverse races and functioning as symbols of the dominant culture.

One can see the same process at work in the buildings that other expansionist powers constructed on alien soil. Florid baroque churches In Mexico and Peru, which rose from the ruins of Aztec and Inca temples, declare their allegiance to Spain and the Spanish missionaries who came in the wake of Cortés and Pizarro (see opposite). Monsters like F. W. Stevens' Victoria Terminus in Bombay (see right), an Indo-Gothic railway station completed at the peak of the British Raj, treat indigenous architecture as little more than a plaything, an unequal partner in a synthesis with inappropriate but controlling

WILLIAM THE CONQUEROR AND THE WHITE TOWER

There are some dates that stick in the mind. On 4 July 1776 all men were created equal, with unalienable rights to life, liberty, and the pursuit of happiness. On Easter Monday 1916, Padraic Pearse stood on the steps of the Dublin Post Office and proclaimed Ireland to be a sovereign independent state. On 6 August 1945 the Enola Gay dropped Little Boy on Hiroshima and changed the world for ever. 14 October 1066 is another such key moment, one of the most famous in European history.

ABOVE **1066 and all that. In this scene from the Bayeux Tapestry, Duke William of Normandy (c.1028–87) gets ready to set sail for England and a place in the history books.**

Early on the morning of Saturday, 14 October 1066, the cavalry of Duke William of Normandy engaged King Harold's Saxon footsoldiers outside the town of Hastings. By nightfall Harold was dead, William had conquered, and the Normans controlled England.

Except that in reality events are never that simple. The important question is always, "What happened next?" With the Battle of Hastings, what happened next was not a victory parade but a long and savage campaign to subdue the native population. Duke William's troops moved eastwards to secure the Kentish ports before heading north to Canterbury, where William fell sick. When he finally attacked London in November, he was driven back and forced to cross the Thames at Wallingford in Berkshire. It was not until Christmas Day that he was crowned king in Westminster Abbey, after a deputation of Saxon earls and bishops formally offered him the crown.

Even then, the Conquest was far from over. There was a revolt in Kent in 1067, and another in the West Country. The following year, the north of England rebelled, and in January 1069 William's representative in Durham was killed and his army of occupation butchered. Two of Harold's sons attacked Devon that summer, while Saxon earls supported by a considerable Danish force, sacked York and consequently provoked risings in the counties of Cheshire, Shropshire, and Staffordshire. William suppressed the northern insurrections with incredible ferocity, laying waste to whole tracts of countryside and leaving corpses to rot by the wayside. "Wholesale massacre," was how one contemporary chronicler described it: "an act which levelled both the bad and the good in one common ruin."

Although sporadic fighting continued for some time, the Norman invaders steadily established themselves as rulers. English earls, bishops,

and sheriffs were removed from office and replaced by Normans. The English language was supplanted by Norman French in court circles and by Latin in legal writs and charters. English dissidents were suppressed, and English culture was simply disregarded.

How was this possible? How could an army of thousands subjugate and control a native population which may have numbered as many as two and a half million? An efficient military organization was the key, and the supreme architectural expression of this organization was the castle. Until the Conquest castles were quite a rarity in England. The Saxons depended instead on a system of burghs or boroughs, communal fortifications rather than purpose-built residential garrisons. Duke William, on the other hand, was well acquainted with the castle's strategic role in warfare from his campaigns in Gaul. He brought over a prefabricated timber castle and erected it at Pevensey in Kent as soon as he landed there at the end of September 1066. And when his soldiers arrived in Hastings a few days later, almost the first thing they did was to build another castle, a motte (or man-made mound) topped by a bailey (an encircling timber palisade).

ABOVE **Although the White Tower has undergone various changes since the 11th century – the windows have been enlarged, for example, and the corner-turrets capped with cupolas – it is still easy to appreciate the impact that it must have had on the citizens of London.**

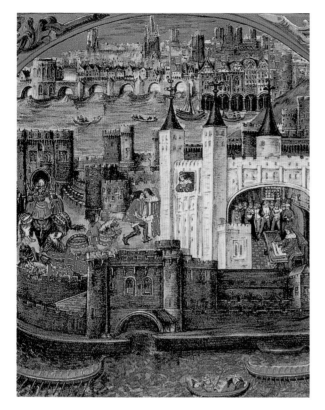

ABOVE **An illustration showing London and the White Tower in the 15th century. The Tower takes its name from the fact that it was originally whitewashed with a mixture of powdered chalk and water.**

OPPOSITE **The chapel of St John, in the Tower. "Whenever his health permitted," wrote a contemporary obituarist, William "regularly and with great piety, attended Christian Worship each morning and evening and at the celebration of mass."**

The motte-and-bailey was by far the most common form of fortification in the immediate aftermath of the Conquest. No-one knows for sure how many were built as the invaders moved west and north, but the figure is likely to number well into the thousands. Some were thrown up quickly as a response to an isolated pocket of resistance, and soon dismantled. Others – permanent garrisons in strategic trouble-spots – were much more elaborate affairs, measuring up to 27 metres (90 feet) in height with ancillary buildings in the surrounding fenced-in bailey and ditches faced with timber to make them harder to climb. And they were big; at York one-seventh of the city was razed to clear space for castle-works at the time of the 1069 rising; while in Lincoln around the same time, 160 houses were destroyed to make way for the conquerors' new castle.

As the largest city in the country, London was provided with two castles very early on; William felt insecure without the protection they afforded against the English. According to his biographer, William of Poitiers, the King retreated to Barking in Essex straight after his coronation, "while certain strongholds were made in the city against the fickleness of the vast and fierce population." One of these strongholds may have been Baynards Castle in the west of the city, long since gone. The other, to the east, was the first Tower of London.

Nothing much is known about the first castle on the site. William's engineers secured the perimeter by enclosing it within old Roman walls to the south and east and digging ditches to the north and west. No doubt there were also timber palisades and earth ramparts, and perhaps some rough-and-ready ancillary structures within the bailey surrounding the main building. But by about 1078 the King had become dissatisfied with this arrangement, and ordered that it be replaced with an altogether more imposing fortress-palace. This was the White Tower, which stands at the heart of the present-day Tower of London. (It derives its name from the fact that, at one time, its exterior walls were plastered and whitewashed.) The supervisor of the new works was Gundulf, a monk from Caen in Normandy, who became Bishop of Rochester in 1077 and whose interest in architecture – contemporaries reckoned him "very competent and skilful at building in stone" – led to at least two further projects: Colchester Castle in Essex (which bears a strong resemblance to the London castle) and a new cathedral for his own diocese.

Together with Colchester, the White Tower is the earliest stone keep in England. The native population were completely unfamiliar with stone building on this scale, and it must have come as quite a culture-shock to them – no doubt the King's intention. Its plan is a simple rectangle 36 metres by 30 metres (118 feet by 97 feet), excluding a semi-circular projection to the south-east and four corner turrets; and it rises to an impressive 27 metres (90 feet) at battlement level.

Inside its 4.6 metre- (15 foot-) thick walls there were three storeys, each divided into three compartments. Above a self-contained raised basement, with a well to provide an independent water supply in case of attack, were the constable's lodgings, reached via an easily defended external wooden staircase. The main floor of state was at the top of the tower, open to the rafters and indicating its status by being almost twice the height of the constable's lodgings below. Occupying the whole of the western half was a great hall with a

central hearth, the main living room in the castle and the architectural expression of the King's presence. We know nothing of its appearance, but it was probably quite colourful, with whitewashed or colourwashed walls and perhaps some simple painted or stencilled decoration.

To the east of the hall lay the King's private chamber – as private as chambers came, anyway, in an age when personal servants slept on straw pallets both inside and outside their master's door. Adjoining it was the chapel of St John (see left), the east end of which terminates in an apse to form the projection mentioned earlier. A chapel was an integral part of all royal and noble households, but it was particularly important to William, whose religiosity was frequently noted by contemporary chroniclers. Although it has long since lost the brightly painted ornament that once decorated its walls, the chapel remains remarkably intact – austere, forbidding, and one of the great survivals of Norman ecclesiastical architecture in Britain.

William I died at Rouen in September 1087, some years before the White Tower was finished, and it was left to William Rufus to complete the project and to replace his father's timber and earth perimeter with stone walls. Other kings and queens made their own contributions, and nowadays the White Tower is only one element in the complex of later buildings that make up the Tower of London. It is hard to appreciate the impact it must have had in the 1080s, as it grew inexorably, stone by stone, until it dominated the city, although the fact that the complex is still known as the Tower rather than the Castle of London is an indication of how potent a symbol the Conqueror's building was. As a royal residence and the adminstrative headquarters of government, it had a utilitarian, practical function. But above and beyond this it was a symbol in stone of Norman authority, a signal to the English that their conquerors were here to stay.

KUBILAI KHAN
AND BEIJING

When Marco Polo arrived at the court of Kubilai Khan in 1275, he was astounded. The roofs of the Khan's great palace at Ta-tu glittered like crystal in the sun, scarlet and green and blue and yellow. Kings and princes from Baghdad to Korea acknowledged him as their lord. Prominent nobles lined up to hand over their daughters for service as his concubines. It was obvious that "this Great Khan is the mightiest man... who is in the world today or who ever has been."

ABOVE **Marco Polo recalled the face of Kubilai Khan (c.1215–94) as "fair and ruddy like a rose, the eyes black and handsome, the nose shapely and set square in place."**

RIGHT **The Mongol Emperor laid out Ta-tu on traditional Confucian lines – to evoke China's past and show the native people that their new leader was a true Son of Heaven.**

The mightiest man in the world had then been ruling over most of Asia for 15 years. He was a grandson of the legendary Chingiz or Genghis Khan, the chieftain of a minor clan on the Mongolian steppes who had risen to rule an empire that stretched from the Volga to the Pacific, and from the forests of Siberia to the borders of Iran. In the decades following the death of Chingiz in 1227, his offspring extended his dominions still further, using a lethal combination of brilliant military tactics and terrifying brutality. In the west, Mongol cavalry swept through Russia, Hungary, and Poland, devastating Kiev and coming within striking distance of Vienna. In the Middle East their armies looted Baghdad, butchering hundreds of thousands of its population before marching into Damascus, where the massacre lasted for six days. In the Far East, they moved into the jungles of Indo-China, destroyed the capital of Burma, launched a seaborne assault on Japan, and occupied Java. By the later 13th century the Mongols ruled over the largest contiguous land empire that history has ever seen. Little wonder that Marco Polo was impressed.

One of Chingiz's first military forays outside the Mongols' traditional homelands had been across the Gobi Desert into China, where his forces razed more than 90 cities, left the capital burning for a month, and ruthlessly subdued the Jurchens, who controlled the northern parts of China at the time. He considered slaughtering the whole population and turning the country over to pasture, until his advisers pointed out that there was more to be gained from taxing the inhabitants than from grazing his horses in the ruins of their farms. After Kubilai succeeded to the Great Khanate in 1260, he continued the Mongol thrust southwards into the empire of the Sung, who controlled the southern half of China. In 1276, when the Sung capital of Hangzhou capitulated in the face of the Khan's threat to put to death every one of its million inhabitants – something he had already done in the Sung city of Changzhou – the northern and southern halves of the country were reunited for the first time in three centuries.

In the 1260s Kubilai deserted his capital, Karakorum in Mongolia. His summer residence was at Shang-tu (Coleridge's Xanadu) on the Chinese border; and during the winter months he lived in the old Jurchen capital at Beijing. In 1272 he took two further steps towards confirming China as his powerbase. The first was to announce that the Mongol dynasty had adopted the title of

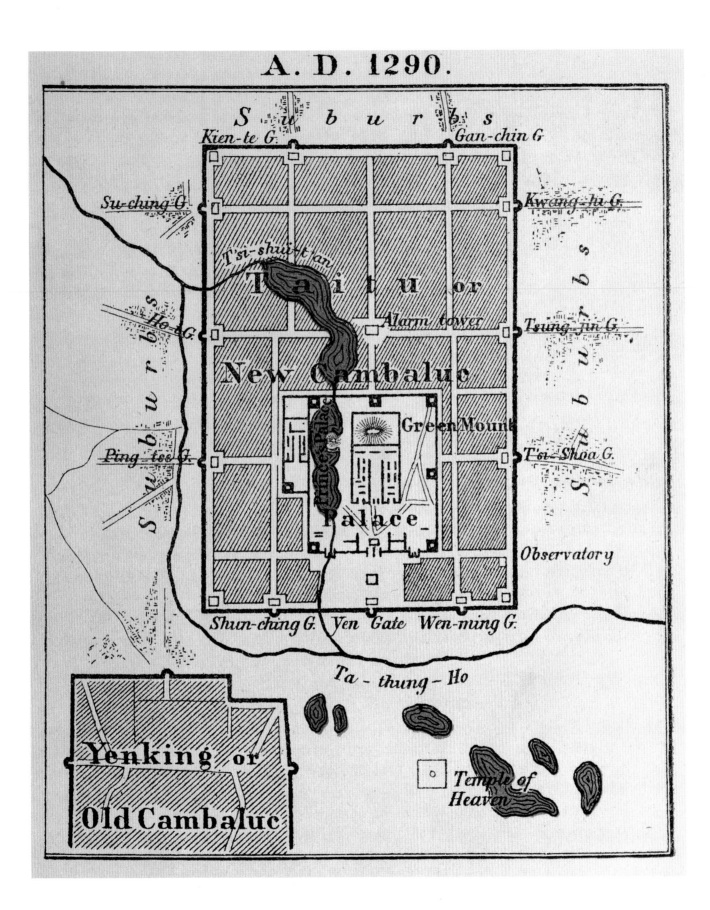

A.D. 1290.

"Yuan," which in Mandarin means "the origin" – a move intended to inform the native Chinese that Kubilai was now a Son of Heaven and thus their legitimate ruler, rather than merely the head of an occupying force. The second was to declare that his winter residence, which had been rebuilt on his orders between 1267 and 1271, was henceforth to be known as Ta-tu – "the great capital."

Ta-tu was built in the form of a square with a perimeter nearly 10 kilometres (16 miles) round. Great earthen walls some 12 metres (40 feet) high and 6 metres (20 feet) wide at their base tapered up to narrow battlemented walkways, with four corner towers and twelve high gatehouses, three on each side. Ta-tu was laid out on a grid, with broad straight streets and regular blocks containing houses, inns and shops. In the exact centre of the city a bell-tower sounded curfew the each night. Below it, to the south, was

"All the treasures that come from India – precious stones, pearls, and other rarities – are brought here. So too are the choicest and costliest products of Cathay itself and every other province... every day more than one thousand cart-loads of silk enter the city..." MARCO POLO

Kubilai's heavily guarded palace, a vast complex of brightly painted wooden pavilions surrounded by ornamental gardens and set within two concentric square enclosures. The main entrance was 26 metres (85 feet) high and 57 metres (187 feet) wide, flanked by two crenellated towers connected to thhe main block by covered walkways, and topped with a series of fortified lookout turrets. Inside the complex there was a series of halls and chambers, their interior walls decorated with murals of battle-scenes, birds, and mythical beasts, their ceilings covered with gold and silver.

The splendours of Kubilai's Ta-tu were totally alien to European eyes. But the new capital of the Mongol Empire would not have seemed so

strange to the conquered population. With its emphasis on harmony (a centrally placed palace with symmetrical facades, a carefully ordered layout with straight vistas and geometrically disposed housing) its architecture represents a rigidly classical interpretation of early Confucian practices. Although only fragments of Ta-tu survive, contemporary descriptions by both Europeans and Chinese show that it closely followed the pattern prescribed in the *Chou li*, the ancient Chinese text on government which stipulated, for example, that a capital should be square, with three gateways on each side, a symmetrical gridwork of avenues and a centrally placed palace – all features to be found in Ta-tu. The city's architects were almost certainly native Chinese, and Kubilai was clearly eager to invoke China's past rather than imposing the victor's culture on a vanquished race.

The Khan's generals and some of his nomadic kinsmen in Central Asia and Mongolia viewed his urbanization with suspicion, even hostility; rather than live under a roof, they erected their painted tents or *gers* in the palace grounds. But Kubilai was careful to maintain several degrees of separation between Mongol and native. He forbade intermarriage between the two races, barred the Chinese from learning the Mongol language or carrying weapons, and completely excluded the Confucian literati (the traditional administrative class) from the civil service, preferring instead to rely on Muslim, Buddhist, and Christian outsiders.

As far as the architectural character of Ta-tu is concerned, the Khan's adoption of Chinese forms is not so surprising. When Kubilai was born around 1215, permanent Mongol architecture was virtually non-existent. He had no familar vernacular styles to import, as did the Romans and the Normans when they invaded Britain – unless, like his generals, he had been content to live in a timber *ger* with felt walls. The administrative

ABOVE **Marco Polo and his father Niccolo are presented to the "mightiest man in the world." The illustration is taken from a 14th-century manuscript, one of the many medieval versions of Polo's account of his visit to the Khan's court.**

headquarters of a great empire required permanence, and his models were Chinese models; his craftsmen were Chinese craftsmen.

Kubilai could have taken over existing Jurchen buildings in Beijing, but he needed a statement of power and a new beginning. As the new capital of a newly reunited China, and the seat of the new Yuan dynasty, Ta-tu's severe Confucianism looked back to pre-Jurchen times, as if to say that *they* had been the usurpers. The Great Khan was not an invader, he was ruling by the mandate of Heaven and restoring China to its former glory.

As an instrument of statecraft, Kubilai Khan's city of Ta-tu was an immensely sophisticated piece of work, especially for one whose grandparents had ranged over the Mongolian steppes with their horses, carrying their possessions. Architecture was used to win the respect of a vanquished population and to legitimize a new ruler. Moreover, its incredible opulence made Ta-tu one of the wonders of the world. But it was destined to be a short-lived wonder. In 1368 the last Yuan emperor was overthrown by Zhu Yuanzhang, the founder of the Ming dynasty, who made Nanjing his capital. But in the early 1400s the Ming emperors moved to Ta-tu, replacing Kubilai's buildings and creating the Forbidden City on the site. Today there are only a few scattered remnants – and Marco Polo's *Travels* – to tell us about the legendary city built by the mightiest man in the world.

EDWARD I AND HIS WELSH CASTLES

"Father of treachery, child of rebellion, son of iniquity, author of sedition, patron of ingratitude, convict of perjury and head of all evil": Llywelyn ap Gruffydd was not a popular figure at the court of Edward I. Not that the Welsh Prince was a regular visitor; Llywelyn's refusal to pay homage in person to Edward was one of the reasons why the King ordered a general muster of arms at Worcester in 1277, with a view to administering a stern rebuke to the Welsh.

ABOVE **Edward I (1239–1307) is seated on the right in this medieval manuscript. His second campaign against the Welsh (1282–3) resulted in the annexation of Wales.**

The argument had been rumbling on since 1274, when Edward returned from crusading in the Holy Land to be crowned king. According to the Treaty of Montgomery, which Llywelyn had concluded with Henry III seven years previously, the Welsh Prince was recognized as overlord of north and west Wales, and in return he agreed to acknowledge the English King as his lord and to make annual payments to the Crown. But now Llywelyn was angry at English incursions into territory that was his according to the treaty; he was unwilling (and possibly unable) to continue the heavy annual payments; and he had grave doubts about Edward's offers of safe conduct on English soil.

There followed a farcical series of failed rendezvous. Llywelyn agreed to come to Shrewsbury to pay homage in November 1274, but Edward was ill and could not attend. The following August, Edward turned up at Chester, but Llywelyn did not. Then Edward issued a series of summonses for the Welsh Prince to appear at Westminster in October 1275, at Winchester in January 1276, and at Westminster again that April. Llywelyn refused, and in November Edward finally lost his patience, declared Llywelyn a rebel and a disturber of the King's peace, and announced his intention to go to war.

The expeditionary force that Edward called to Worcester in July 1277 moved north to Chester, before advancing along the north Wales coast to Anglesey. They met with little resistance, and by November Llywelyn, who was trapped in his mountain stronghold of Snowdonia with his supplies cut off, agreed to a humiliating peace. Matters did not end there, however. English attempts to replace Welsh laws and customs and Edward's perceived failure to reward those Welsh nobles who had supported him in 1277 led to widespread resentment. At Easter 1282 war broke out once more when, without warning, Llywelyn's brother Dafydd stormed Hawarden Castle a few miles west of Chester. Within days the Welsh had launched attacks on other English-held castles at Oswestry, Aberystwyth, Carreg Cennen, and Llandovery. Again Edward mobilized his army.

This time the King was determined not merely to teach the Welsh a lesson, but to conquer them. An army of around 9000 men – roughly three times the size of the 1277 force – was mustered at Rhuddlan and, in spite of suffering several heavy defeats, Edward steadily gained control of north Wales, pushing the Welsh back into Snowdonia. Llywelyn tried to break out before his forces were completely encircled, marching down into central Wales in November; he was killed in a skirmish outside Builth on 11 December. His brother Dafydd sued for peace, but the offer was rejected, and Edward prepared for a long fight – even to the extent of equipping some of his troops with white tunics as camouflage for a winter war in the mountains. That fight lasted until the following June, two months after the fall of the last Welsh stronghold, Castell-y-Bere, when Prince Dafydd was captured. He was later executed – if "execution" is the right word for a process that involved being dragged through the streets by horses, being hanged, having one's bowels burned, and finally being dismembered.

With Dafydd dead, and various parts of him on display in towns all over England, Welsh resistance to Edward all but came to an end. The Plantagenet King had learned well from his Norman predecessors; like them, he established

BELOW **Harlech Castle formed part of Edward's "Iron Ring" of fortifications that encircled north Wales. The area was taken by English foot-soldiers in April 1823; within weeks an army of royal masons was at work.**

they who threw a great wall around the complex, ordered the construction of many of the towers that guard it, and built an aqueduct to supply the citadel with water from further up the mountain.

They presumably also had a royal residence on the hilltop, but the Alhambra's golden age really belongs to Yûsuf I (reigned 1333–54) and his successor, Muhammad V, who was known as Al-Ghani-billah ("the rich in God"). Yûsuf demolished many of the earlier buildings, creating in their stead the Comares Palace, a group of state rooms and private lodgings arranged in the usual Islamic fashion around an open rectangular court (known today as the Myrtle Court because of its borders of myrtle), with a formal pool at its centre. The pinnacle of Yûsuf's palace was his throne room, the Hall of the Ambassadors, which occupies the Comares Tower at the northern end of the court. Here, beneath a magnificent seven-

tiered ceiling emblazoned with thousands of inlaid wooden stars, the Sultan received emissaries from Castile, from the Christian nobles who held territory along Granada's frontiers, and from the Muslim Marinids of North Africa – all allies of the politically adept Nasrids at one time or another.

Death came unexpectedly to Yûsuf. One day in 1354 the Sultan was making the last prostration of his prayers in the citadel mosque when a madman broke through his bodyguard and thrust a dagger into his back. As the assassin was tossed to the infuriated mob outside the doors of the mosque to be lynched and burned, Yûsuf was carried to his lodgings to die, leaving as his successor Muhammad V.

Such a beginning to a reign was hardly propitious; but Muhammad's problems had only just started. The first few years of his sultanate were

CHAPTER 3

RENAISSANCE

That is easy enough to say when you already have the grandeur and fame, the piazzas and temples, and magnificent buildings. Although his traditional role as the moving force behind the High Renaissance has been downgraded by historians over recent years (he used to be credited with single-handedly discovering Botticelli, Leonardo, and Michelangelo), Lorenzo's active interest in architecture is beyond dispute. He was called on to arbitrate on various city schemes, is known to have submitted a design to the competition for the uncompleted facade of the cathedral in 1491, and one of his dearest possessions was a manuscript of Alberti's *De re aedificatoria*, the first architectural treatise of the Renaissance. He also wanted to create a completely new layout for the streets of Florence, "to make the city greater and more beautiful" – and, he might have added, more uniform and regular. He was only prevented by the fact that even a Medici was not in a position to impose his will so dramatically on the property-owning classes.

In 1494, two years after Lorenzo's early death, his grandfather's prophecy was borne out, when the Medici were ejected from Florence in a popular rising led by the puritanical Dominican Girolamo Savonarola. The Palazzo Medici was looted, and the Signoria appropriated the bank's assets and the family's fabulous collection of pictures, statues, cameos, and medals.

Savonarola's regime proved more short-lived than the Medici's; in 1498 he was burned alive for heresy in the Piazza della Signoria. Giovanni and Giuliano de' Medici, Lorenzo's surviving sons, returned to the city in 1512, only to be ousted again in 1527 by a pro-republican population that mistrusted their increasingly autocratic regime. It took military intervention in 1530 by the armies of the Holy Roman Emperor Charles V and Pope Clement VII (who happened to be Lorenzo the Magnificent's nephew) to restore them, and this time it was official. Alessandro, great-grandson of

"I know the humours of my city. Before 50 years have passed, we shall be expelled. But my buildings will remain." COSIMO DE' MEDICI

Lorenzo, was made Duke of Florence by Pope Clement; and 40 years later the Medici became grand dukes of Tuscany, ruling the ex-Republic for another two centuries.

It was during the troubled years of the 1520s and 1530s that the Medici made what many regard as their greatest single contribution to the architecture of the Renaissance. In around 1491, Lorenzo the Magnificent had intended to build a new sacristy at San Lorenzo, to balance the old sacristy. Plans were shelved when he died the following year, but when Giovanni and Giuliano came back to Florence they commissioned Michelangelo to take up the work as a funerary chapel for the family (see p.67).

The result is quite simply one of the most beautiful spaces in the world, and one of the first with the confidence to extend the classical canon by breaking the rules. Even Vasari, whose respect for Michelangelo knew no bounds, was uneasy at the variety of ornament that was not sanctioned by classical tradition, a complicated arrangement of slender pilasters and triangular and segmental pediments in white marble and grey *pietra serena* – although he did admit that "artisans have been infinitely and perpetually indebted to him because he broke the bonds and chains of a way of working that had become habitual." A high vaulted cube, the dome of which was the first to emulate the ceiling of Hadrian's Pantheon in Rome, towers over the monuments to Giuliano Medici and his nephew Lorenzo – ironically, two of the least distinguished members of the family.

Michelangelo left Florence in 1534, and the tombs of Lorenzo the Magnificent and his brother were never executed. Their grandfather Cosimo lies beneath the dome in the nave of the church, as discreet in death as he was in life.

RIGHT **The opulently decorated interior of the family chapel at the Palazzo Medici. Benozzo Gozzoli's murals of the journey of the Magi to Bethlehem, begun in 1459, incorporate several members of the Medici family, including Cosimo the Elder and a young Lorenzo the Magnificent.**

FRANCIS I AND FONTAINEBLEAU

Francis I cannot have had much time for architecture. He was too busy chasing women. According to stories that circulated after his death, the French King had an incestuous relationship with his sister, pursued his guardian's widow Mary Tudor, caught syphilis from a mistress and gave it to his first wife (who died as a result), and seduced one of his mother's ladies-in-waiting. As one contemporary so picturesquely put it, the King "breaks into others' gardens and drinks at many sources."

ABOVE **Francis I (1494–1547), warrior-prince, discerning patron of the arts, and sexual obsessive, is shown in this portrait (c.1535) by François Clouet, court painter to several French kings.**

Some of the tales about Francis's hectic sex-life were either wild exaggerations or plain lies. But there was enough truth in them to bear out what courtiers said of the King – that while Alexander the Great saw women when he had no business, "Francis attends to business when there are no women." Fortunately for us, however, the King did find time for other less transient pleasures. He came to the throne in 1515, and right at the beginning of his reign he brought Leonardo da Vinci and Andrea del Sarto to France. Leonardo died in 1519 without much to show for three years in the King's service, while Andrea painted only one picture before decamping to his native Florence, where he promptly spent all the money the King had given him for paintings and sculptures. This seems to have temporarily dampened Francis's enthusiasm for collecting artists, but from the late 1520s onwards a steady stream of craftsmen were invited to work at the French court. The brilliant but neurotic painter Giovanni Battista Rosso – "Il Fiorentino" – arrived from Venice in 1530 and stayed until his suicide in 1540; he was followed in 1532 by the painter, sculptor, and interior decorator Francesco Primaticcio. The sculptor Benvenuto Cellini came in 1537 and again in 1540, staying in the

King's service for five years; the Bolognese architects Sebastiano Serlio and Giacomo Barozzi da Vignola both arrived in 1541. And where he couldn't acquire the artists themselves, Francis went to great lengths to obtain their art. (Given his reputation, it comes as no surprise to learn he was eager to acquire erotic nudes.) In his whole-hearted espousal of the cultural values of the Renaissance – he talked with Italian artists in their own language, collected antique sculpture, and liked to be depicted as a Roman emperor – he showed he had learned a great political lesson: that the conspicuous display of art enhanced a monarch's status as effectively as military might.

Francis was just as active in the field of architecture as he was in the other arts, although he initially relied on native-born talent. In the Loire, he remodelled Amboise, added a striking double loggia to his wife's chateau at Blois (1515–24), and built an entirely new chateau at Chambord (1519–47; see pp.60–61 and 63). Most of his work at Amboise, which was presumably designed by French masons, has long since vanished. The Façade des Loggias at Blois was probably also by French masons, although they may have been working from drawings or reports of Bramante's recently completed San Damaso courtyard in the

Vatican; it borrows Bramante's basic idea – two tiers of open arches separated by pilasters and topped with a third row of flat-headed openings divided by columns – but not the architect's symmetry and harmony of proportion. Chambord is much more revolutionary, particularly in the symmetrical plan of its main block, which is divided by a Greek cross into four square sets of lodgings on each of three floors, with a spiral staircase in the centre. This plan recalls Lorenzo the Magnificent's villa at Poggio a Caiano, designed by the Florentine architect Giuliano da Sangallo in 1485; it was probably the work of Sangallo's assistant, Domenico da Cortona – another Italian import to the French court – although there is a persistent tradition that Leonardo himself contributed to it in some unspecified way.

Francis's long-suffering first queen, Claude de France, died in 1524 (although probably not of syphilis as was rumoured). After a brief hiatus, the King began a second burst of building activity in 1528. He ordered alterations to the Louvre, where the medieval keep was demolished, and the construction of a new chateau in the Bois de Boulogne. Four years later another chateau was begun at Villers-Cotterêts in the forest of Compiègne north of Paris; and in 1539 work began on the rebuilding of Saint-Germain-en-Laye to the north-west of the capital. But from the early 1530s the King's favourite residence was Fontainebleau, in the forests 50 kilometres (30

ABOVE **The new range of state-rooms at Fontainebleau were designed by Gilles Le Breton and begun in 1528. The court became known as the Cour du Cheval Blanc ("Court of the White Horse"), from a copy of the equestrian statue of Marcus Aurelius in Rome that was placed here in the 18th century.**

"It is the finest house in Christendom: so rich and fair a building, and so large and spacious, that one might house a small world in it." PIERRE BRANTÔME, COURTIER AND WRITER

miles) south of Paris. This was "the finest house in Christendom," according to Pierre Brantôme: "so rich and fair a building, and so large and spacious, that one might house a small world in it."

There had been a royal castle at Fontainebleau since the early Middle Ages. In 1528 Francis commissioned the Parisian mason Gilles Le Breton to modernize the old apartments, which were grouped around an oval courtyard, and to extend the complex by building a huge new courtyard to the west. A passageway which had linked the royal apartments in the castle keep to the monastic church which formerly stood on the site of the new courtyard was converted into a three-storey wing. The ground floor contained a suite of baths. According to the English ambassador, who visited in 1540, they were kept so warm and steamy "like it had been a mist," that Francis had to guide him through them – a fact that makes all the more bizarre the King's decision to keep his most prized paintings there.

Above the baths – and below the attic storey, which housed the King's library – was the Galerie François Ier. This is perhaps the greatest surviving monument to Francis's taste and to the famous First School of Fontainebleau, as Rosso, Primatticcio, and the other Italians who gathered to decorate the palace are generally known. As it

stands today, the palace is not particularly distinguished. This is partly because of Francis's decision to extend the existing medieval layout rather than starting from scratch, making a more cohesive and symmetrical treatment impossible; with its mixture of hard grey stone and red brick, and its courts of different shapes and sizes, the building rambles in a way that must have seemed crass to the purists of the Renaissance. A second reason for its failure is that Le Breton was no great shakes as a designer – although, to be fair, the piecemeal development of the palace during Francis's reign meant that different architects brought different perspectives. Serlio, for example, was put in charge of the works in 1541; and it has also been suggested that Rosso, who was primarily employed on interior decoration, may have played an unspecified role in the evolving design during the 1530s. But the main reason is the alteration of various parts of Fontainebleau by later generations, which led Stendhal to call it a "dictionary of architecture"; it might less charitably be called a muddle. The greatest loss was the Galerie d'Ulysse, a grand vaulted reception hall with 60 murals by Primatticcio and the Modenese

ABOVE **The Ballroom at Fontainebleau was begun in the year of Francis I's death, 1547, and completed by his son, Henry II. It contains scenes depicting the goddess Diana, a reference to Diane de Poitiers, who was mistress to both father and son.**

LEFT **A staircase designed c.1630 by Jacques Androuet du Cerceau. Fontainebleau is much altered since Francis I's time. With a few exceptions, such as du Cerceau's stair, most of these changes have been for the worse.**

OPPOSITE **The Galerie François Ier – a monument to the taste of Francis I and to Primaticcio, Rosso, and the other Italian artists of the First School of Fontainebleau.**

painter Niccolò dell'Abate, which invited parallels between the King and the Homeric hero. It occupied most of the first floor of the south wing in the new chateau, and was destroyed when Louis XV rebuilt the wing in the 18th century. Primaticcio's sensuous murals in the retiring rooms of the King's suite of baths were also destroyed, this time by Louis XIV, who should have known better.

But enough of the original work remains for us to understand why Brantôme called Fontainebleau "the finest house in Christendom." There is Le Breton's Porte Dorée, the three-storey gatehouse to the old castle, which acknowledges its debt to Renaissance classicism in two pilastered loggias flanked by curious stacks of narrow pedimented windows; the elongated and frankly erotic stucco figures that support Primaticcio's equally erotic frescoes in the bedroom of the King's mistress, the Duchesse d'Etampes; and the Galerie François Ier itself, where Rosso designed allegories of Francis's reign so obscure that art historians still argue over their meaning today. Painted panels, each surrounded by a bewildering array of distorted stucco figures, glorify the King, portraying him as warrior, as patron of the arts, even as a mighty elephant, complete with an "F" on his forehead. These specific references to Francis are interspersed with images of naked goddesses that seem less relevant.

Francis I died in 1547, although work at Fontainebleau continued under his son, Henry II. Ironically, considering Francis's determination to be a true prince of the Renaissance, the contorted figures at Fontainebleau represent one of the earliest flowerings of mannerism, the late Renaissance style that art historians used to dismiss as a corruption. But while the allegorical frescoes and stucco nymphs may be a long way from the ideals of the early Renaissance, they are a lot more fun. And that, one feels, is a thought that would have appealed to Francis I.

POPE JULIUS III AND THE VILLA GIULIA

Julius III was not a great pope. Elected to the Holy See in February 1550, the elderly churchman took to the trappings of power with a venal gusto. He embraced a lifestyle well beyond the means of the papal exchequer, flagrantly promoted the interests of his family (no fewer than five of whom were made cardinals), held lavish entertainments for his friends and hangers-on, and scandalized Rome by his relationship with a 15-year-old youth, inappropriately named Innocenzo.

ABOVE **Pope Julius III (1487–1555) is shown in this painting giving an audience to Ottavio Farnese, Duke of Parma. It was said that "In the important affairs of the church and state he took no other share than was absolutely inevitable."**

To a certain extent, by behaving with the cheery disdain of a secular prince who answered to no-one – in this world at least – Julius was acting no differently to many of his illustrious forebears. His immediate predecessor Paul III, for example, had ruthlessly furthered the interests of his own family, the Farnese, and had spent so much on buildings and works of art that by the time of his death the papal exchequer was massively in debt. But Paul was a shrewd and able statesman, and much of his patronage of the arts was directed towards enhancing the prestige of the papacy rather than furthering his own reputation. He commissioned Michelangelo's *Last Judgement* for the Sistine Chapel, and pushed ahead with the rebuilding of St Peter's (which had come to a virtual standstill under the previous two popes). He also took steps to preserve the ruins of the city's classical monuments and began the renovation of the area around the Capitol, the historic political and religious centre of Rome. Paul was keen to exploit the connection between Rome, the ancient capital of empire, and Rome, the seat of the one true church. By linking the two in the popular imagination, he was at once affirming the papacy as the natural successor to the great emperors of the past, and claiming ownership of the two most significant sets of cultural values in Renaissance society – antiquity and Christianity.

Julius III also saw the value of the connection with a great imperial tradition; but the difference was that he saw himself, rather than the institution of the papacy, as the heir. Although he continued several of Paul's building projects, he devoted much more of his time to his own schemes, remodelling his family palace, creating a family chapel in the church of San Pietro in Monterio and – undoubtedly the highlight of his less than sparkling career – building the Villa Giulia, a *villa suburbana* on what is now the Via delle Belle Arti in Rome.

The design of the Villa Giulia and its gardens was a collaborative effort. Like many wealthy patrons of the time, Julius himself played an active part, outlining his ideas to his kinsman, the painter-architect Giorgio Vasari. Vasari would sketch out the Pope's ideas, and take them to

Michelangelo, who advised him and suggested improvements. The amended drawings would then go for further revisions to the principal architect, Giacomo Barozzi da Vignola, who at some point early on in the proceedings was joined by yet another designer, Bartolommeo Ammannati. To complicate matters further, during the three or four years when building was in progress – the villa was begun in 1551 and more or less completed by the time of the Pope's death – Julius frequently changed his mind over this detail or that, much to the irritation of everyone involved; while his agent for the works, the papal chamberlain Pier Giovanni Aliotti, was also eager to retain some degree of control over the whole business, and constantly interfered. (Michelangelo found this particularly exasperating, referring to him as "Busybody.")

Not surprisingly, it is difficult to disentangle individual contributions in such a convoluted process. Vasari, whose *Lives of the Artists* is the major documentary source for the building history of the Villa Giulia, is not a particularly reliable witness; as a distant relation of the Pope and a devoted admirer of Michelangelo, he was obviously keen to talk up their roles – and, of course, his own. Against this, the villa was the first major commission for both Vignola, who like many

BELOW **The garden facade of the Villa Giulia; Julius's retreat is enclosed within the arms of Vignola's sweeping portico, keeping his private pleasures safe from the eyes of the world.**

which looks onto a long courtyard. The reference – which may have come from Julius himself – is to one of the most famous villas of antiquity, Pliny the Younger's seaside estate at Laurentinum; Pliny's account of the villa, in which he talks of "an atrium at the entrance, simple but not drab, then a porticus in the shape of the letter "D" which surrounds a small but cheerful court," was well known in the 16th century. But apart from deliberately conjuring up associations with first-century Rome, the design relies for its effect on surprise. The contrast between the austerity of the entrance and the grand curves of the garden front – a contrast between public duty and private pleasure, one might be tempted to say, if Julius hadn't taken so little trouble to do his public duty or to keep his pleasures private – is startling, deliberately lowering the visitor's expectations, only to raise them again with a breathtaking suddenness. And this element of surprise continues down the long main axis. Vignola's colonnade, which carries the second storey of the building above it, is extended with single-storey screen walls so that the courtyard is enclosed on both sides. It terminates in another straight facade, which completely conceals from view a second court, probably designed by Ammannati. This echoes the "D"-shaped geometry of Vignola's colonnade, with two curving flights of steps that take the visitor down to a sunken terrace, in the centre of which is a third "D" – a nymphaeum or water-garden that lies at an even lower level and is reached by stairways hidden in the walls (see opposite). Statues look out from niches; marble caryatids support the terrace above; the floor is decorated with a classical mosaic; and water flows from the Acqua Vergine, the aqueduct which Agrippa brought to Rome for his famous baths in the first century BC and which Julius restored and diverted to the grounds of his new villa. A portico beyond the nymphaeum leads to the final area in the axial sequence, a private walled garden.

Renaissance architects had trained as a painter (but who would go on from here to become perhaps the greatest architect of the later 16th century), and Ammannati, who was primarily a sculptor. These days Vignola is usually credited with responsibility for the main block, and Ammannati with the garden buildings; but no-one really knows the extent to which Michelangelo, Vasari, or Julius played significant parts in the design process.

Vignola's entrance facade is a restrained, rather severe two-storey block, completely dominated by a frontispiece of three bays with rusticated columns and pilasters, which was clearly intended to evoke memories of the triumphal arch. A central round-headed opening flanked by smaller niches leads into a rectangular atrium, and from there straight out through a second triumphal arch into a sweeping semi-circular loggia

The opulence, the constant references to ancient Rome, and the rather disconcerting absence of Christian imagery all suggest a dedicated sybarite who, with his election to the papacy, was finally free to ditch his day-job and indulge his fantasies of imperial grandeur.

Since 1889 the Villa Giulia has housed the national museum of Etruscan art. Much of the Renaissance decoration has been destroyed, and most of the antique sculptures have long since been removed to the Vatican. It is difficult to imagine the place as it was in Julius's time, when villa, loggias, and nymphaeum were only part of a much larger complex of gardens and avenues that stretched right across to the Tiber. In its heyday the grounds covered a huge area. Thousands of chestnut, elm, myrtle, and cherry trees were planted; there were walks, aviaries, and little woods; and the interiors of the villa itself were filled with allegorical frescoes, grotesques, murals showing scenes from imperial history, and antique statues of gods and emperors.

Impressive though it was (and it was – even at the time, the citizens of Rome were appalled that their Pope could spend such vast sums on a building that was intended for his own personal use),

the Villa Giulia was never really intended as a residence for Julius III. The Vatican was less than 3 kilometres (2 miles) away to the west, and Castel Sant'Angelo was closer still. The villa was primarily a retreat, a giant pleasure-ground where Julius, carried in the papal barge to a specially built harbour on the edge of the estate, could turn his back on the cares of state and get down to the serious business of enjoying himself. The opulence, the constant references to ancient Rome and, when one comes to think about it, the rather disconcerting absence of Christian iconography all suggest a dedicated sybarite who, with his election to the papacy, was finally free to ditch his day-job and indulge his fantasies of imperial grandeur. He once said, "If you knew with how little expenditure of sense the world is governed, you would wonder." To walk through the Villa Giulia, beautiful though it is, is to wonder indeed.

BELOW **The sensuous curves of Ammannati's nymphaeum, a secluded water-garden where Julius could relax with his friends, refer back to Vignola's portico. The recurring "D" motif provides the villa with a unity that belies the fact that it was the work of several architects.**

PHILIP II
AND **THE ESCORIAL**

Philip II is famous for two things. His beard was singed in Francis Drake's daring raid on Cadiz in 1587; and he was the wicked tyrant whose Armada was ignominiously routed by a plucky little English fleet the following year. Traditionally dismissed as a gloomy, bigoted fanatic, blamed for his wife Mary Tudor's loss of Calais to the French, jeered at for his indecisiveness and reviled for his support of the Inquisition, history – English-speaking Protestant history, at least – has not been kind to him.

ABOVE **Rubens' heroic portrait of Philip II of Spain (1527–98) gives no hint that beneath the shining armour beat the heart of a pompous, pious, and pathologically earnest bureaucrat.**

Nor has history been fair. Philip's pious temperament earned him the respect of many of his contemporaries; so did his sense of justice and his determination to do the right thing.

His palace-monastery of the Escorial had its genesis in two acts of piety. On 10 August 1557, St Lawrence's Day, Spanish forces inflicted a massive defeat on the French outside the town of St Quentin in the Somme valley; after the battle Philip vowed that he would one day build a great church in thanksgiving for the victory and dedicate it to St Lawrence. Then in 1558 came the death of his father, the Holy Roman Emperor Charles V; a codicil in his will begged his dutiful son to build a suitable mausoleum for himself and his wife, Isabella of Portugal. Not a man to take lightly either his personal vow to a saint or the dying wish of his father, Philip set about looking for the right site. It had to be close to Madrid, the city he made his capital

in 1560, but far enough away to serve as a retreat from the cares of state. After several false starts, he finally decided on Escorial, a little village on the slopes of the Guadarrama Mountains 50 kilometres (30 miles) north-west of Madrid.

Juan Bautista de Toledo, who had worked on the basilica of St Peter's in Rome and who was currently Philip's viceroy in Naples, was recalled to Spain and appointed as royal architect. Work began on clearing the area in 1562, and the foundation stone was laid the following April. By the time the final stone was set in place, 22 years and six million ducats later, the Escorial had grown from an act of devotion into a grim, grey, granite-and-slate block with towers at each corner, containing within its forbidding walls a vast complex of buildings. There were state apartments, a Hieronymite monastery, a college, and a huge library for the King's collection of Greek, Latin, and Arabic manuscripts. And there was the church itself. The domed basilica of San Lorenzo el Real remained the focal point of the complex. It was placed in the centre, opposite the entrance gate, and reached through the Patio of the Kings, a large courtyard named for the six kings of Judah whose statues looked down from above the doorway of the church.

The traditional explanation for the gridiron plan of the palace is that it was a conceit, an evocation in stone of St Lawrence's martyrdom. (The saint is reputed to have been roasted on a gridiron.) The royal apartments, which project out from the rectangle behind San Lorenzo, are reckoned to represent the handle of the gridiron. More intriguing is the suggestion that Philip was intent on recreating the fabled House of Solomon, which the Bible says was also a complex of inner courtyards grouped around a central temple. But a more immediate source of inspiration was the great hospital in Milan, then part of the Holy Roman Empire which had been ruled over by Charles V. Built in 1456, the Milanese hospital also had a church at its centre and a series of internal courtyards grouped within a rectangle. Philip may well have seen it when he visited Milan in 1548; in any case, the basic layout had already appeared in Spain, most notably in the pilgrims' hostel built by Enrique Egas at Santiago de Compostela in the early 16th century.

The design was in many ways a team effort, like so many Renaissance palaces. The basic idea may have come from Philip, whose desire that the Escorial should express "simplicity of form, severity in the whole, nobility without arrogance, majesty without ostentation" underpins the whole

BELOW **An anonymous bird's-eye view of the Escorial (1563–84), designed by Juan Bautista de Toledo, Francesco Paciotta, Giovanni Battista Castello of Bergamo, and Juan de Herrera. The domed basilica of San Lorenzo el Real is in the centre, with the King's apartments behind it.**

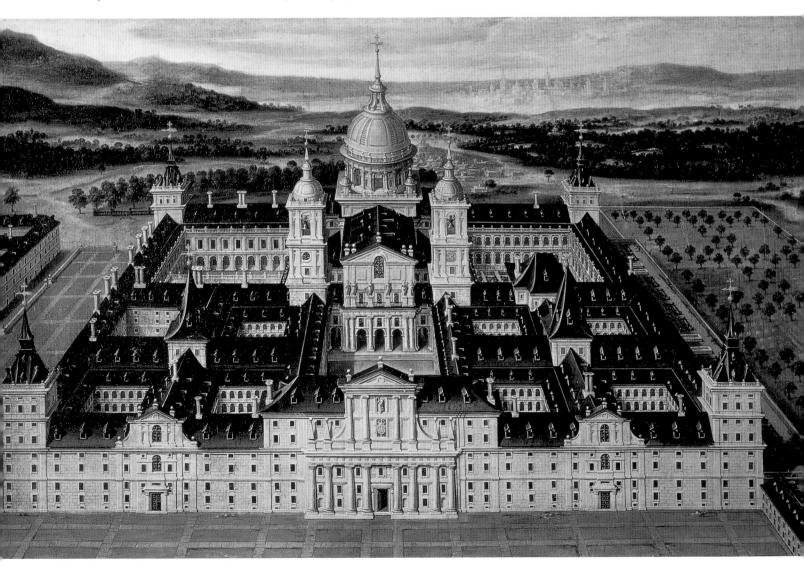

ABOVE **Murals in the Hall of Battles depict Spanish military triumphs. Philip preferred to spend his time in the much more modest surroundings of his sparsely furnished private lodgings.**

OPPOSITE **Philip II built the Escorial in fulfilment of two vows: one was to give thanks for his victory over the French at St Quentin in 1557; and the other to honour the dying wish of his father, Charles V, for a grand mausoleum, shown here. The royal family is buried by the high altar in San Lorenzo.**

scheme. Or it may have come from Bautista de Toledo, who had spent much of his working life in Rome, and who was well able to interpret the King's wishes. It was certainly modified several times in the execution, first by the military engineer Francesco Paciotta, who advised Bautista; then by Giovanni Battista Castello of Bergamo, who took over for two years after Bautista's death in 1567; and finally by Bautista's chief assistant, Juan de Herrera, who effectively became chief architect in 1569.

Philip maintained personal control at every stage. (Personal, that is, in the King's own rather idiosyncratic way; an ardent and reclusive bureaucrat, he preferred whenever possible to communicate by letter, even with his closest officials.) He sketched out his own designs for the entrance facade of the palace, and personally scrutinized and signed all the bills and contracts. Even when he had much weightier matters to occupy him, the Escorial's smallest details were on his mind. When he was busy annexing Portugal in the early 1580s, for example, he still found time to worry over the design of the choir stalls or to get just the right plants for the new gardens. "Ask Enrique, my tailor, the name of the tree that grows by his house," he wrote to one of his officials from Lisbon, "and let me know what it is."

From the beginning, Philip also visited the Escorial in person as often as possible. In the early years of the building work he lodged in the priest's house – the only one in the village with windows and a chimney – and heard mass in a tiny chapel, where his chair of state was a three-legged stool made from a tree-stump. Later he moved to a temporary apartment next door to the monastery, from where he urged on the work – still largely by letter – and wandered the cloisters in his habitual black garb. He was staying there one night in 1577 when lightning set fire to the half-completed palace. As he watched from a courtyard, the workmen desperately fought to contain the blaze while the monks sought to invoke divine aid by waving around the arm of St Lawrence, one of many relics that had found their way to the monastery.

By the time the Escorial was finished it had become a retreat – but a retreat fit for a Renaissance prince. Around and behind the church of San Lorenzo was a network of audience chambers, galleries, and royal apartments which illustrate perfectly Philip's public and private faces. They range in size and opulence from the 54 metre- (177 foot-) long Hall of Battles (see left), decorated with frescoes of Spanish military triumphs, to the King's monastically simple private apartments, with their plain brick floors and whitewashed walls. José de Sigüenza, the monk whom he appointed as official chronicler of the building, noted that he "did not come here to be King, but to be one of the most pious of religious persons." The alcove that contained the King's bed was filled with images of saints; and his personal oratory was fitted with an internal window that looked directly down onto the high altar of San Lorenzo.

"He has no other pleasures, no other contentments, than to live with his monks in his house of San Lorenzo," wrote the Venetian ambassador. Perhaps. Yet whatever Philip's personal inclinations, he was a Renaissance prince, and the most powerful king in Europe. As such, his ability to gather around him the richest, the rarest, the most curious objects and works of art was a means of celebrating his power and prestige, and whatever his personal inclinations, that mattered to Philip in his role as King of Spain. Relics were acquired – not only the arm of St Lawrence, but dozens of assorted bones of saints, a fragment of the True Cross, even a feather from the wing of the Archangel Gabriel. Books and manuscripts from all over Spain and the dominions found a home in the Escorial's library, and paintings and sculptures were both commissioned and collected. The *Garden of Earthly Delights* triptych by Bosch, with its surreal, almost Dalí-esque figures, was a surprising favourite with the King. But there were also works by Titian and El Greco, a stunning life-size Crucifixion in marble by Cellini, and a magnificent group of kneeling gilded bronzes by the Milanese sculptors Leone and Pompeo Leoni for the High Altar of San Lorenzo. These last depict Charles V and his family and Philip with three of his four wives. Mary Tudor, the least successful match, was tactfully omitted.

The church of San Lorenzo was consecrated on 30 August 1595. That night, in spite of being stricken with gout, the ageing King had himself carried up the mountainside to see his whole palace illuminated by oil lamps in celebration. Three years later, and now suffering from cancer, he was carried back from Madrid to the Guadarrama Mountains to end his days in the place he loved best of all. He died in the little bed-chamber, surrounded by saints.

The Escorial is unusual in Renaissance state architecture, just as Philip was unusual among Renaissance statesmen. An immensely powerful king whose religiosity bordered on mania, he blurred the distinction between palace and church in a more unsettling way than any of the popes, so that the Escorial seems never quite sure whether it is an act of devotion or a display of status. Perhaps it is just that power and piety make uneasy bedfellows – a crucial tension which would never enter Philip's rather earnest head.

POPE SIXTUS V AND ROME

The crowd held its breath as, inch by inch, an army of workmen raised an enormous obelisk into position before St Peter's basilica. The huge granite shaft had powerful resonances for Rome, and for the whole Western world. It had once stood in the Circus of Nero, the scene of many early Christian martyrdoms. Tradition said that St Peter himself had been crucified at its foot. Now, on 10 September 1586, it was being raised before the basilica which stood on the site of the Apostle's grave.

ABOVE **Pope Sixtus V (1521–90) tried to make adultery a capital offence, but his cardinals would not stand for it.**

OPPOSITE **A bird's-eye view of Rome (c.1600), from a fresco in the Vatican. St Peter's is in the foreground, with the obelisk that Sixtus V moved from the Circus of Nero. Across the Tiber is the Piazza del Popolo and another of Sixtus's obelisks.**

The operation, directed by the architect Domenico Fontana, was a marvel of engineering. After an expensive year-long project in which the obelisk had been encased in a timber cage and transported on rollers from the site of the Circus 250 metres (820 feet) away, it was finally secured in place by 800 workmen, 140 horses, and 46 winches and cranes. Four days later, on the Feast of the Exaltation of the Cross, it was solemnly dedicated to Christ. The golden ball which crowned it was replaced with a cross; and another inscription was added to those bearing witness to long-dead Roman emperors: "Behold the Cross of the Lord."

The man responsible for this very public conversion of a pagan monument to Christian purposes was the highly principled if unappealing Pope Sixtus V. Elected by the college of cardinals in April 1585, he ruled, like Julius III, for just five years. But there the resemblance ends; Sixtus was energetic where Julius was idle; an ascetic where Julius was a hedonist; a gifted statesman of integrity where Julius was motivated by self-interest. And while Julius devoted most of his short pontificate to creating a pleasant summer palace for himself, Sixtus V devoted his to the rebuilding of Rome.

Sixtus had become a Franciscan monk at the age of 12, and an implacable monastic austerity remained a defining characteristic throughout his career. Imbued with the spirit of the Counter-Reformation, his determination to root out heresy as an Inquisitor in Venice proved too much even for the papal authorities, who recalled him to Rome; but apart from this slight hiccup, he rose up the ecclesiastical ladder until, on the death of Gregory XIII, he was elected to the Holy See. One of his first tasks as pope was to tackle the problem of brigandage in the Roman countryside, and this he did with characteristic vigour, establishing extradition treaties with neighbouring states, instituting a system of rewards for informants, and executing hundreds, if not thousands, of miscreants. He also sought to raise the moral tone of Rome itself, so that it should be a fitting headquarters for the Church. Paedophilia, incest, and abortion were punished by death. Sabbath-breakers could be sent to the galleys, and the vast army of prostitutes who cruised the main streets of Rome were ordered off the major thoroughfares during daylight hours and off any street at all after dusk. The city was certainly better for his reforms. Whether its citizens were happier is another matter.

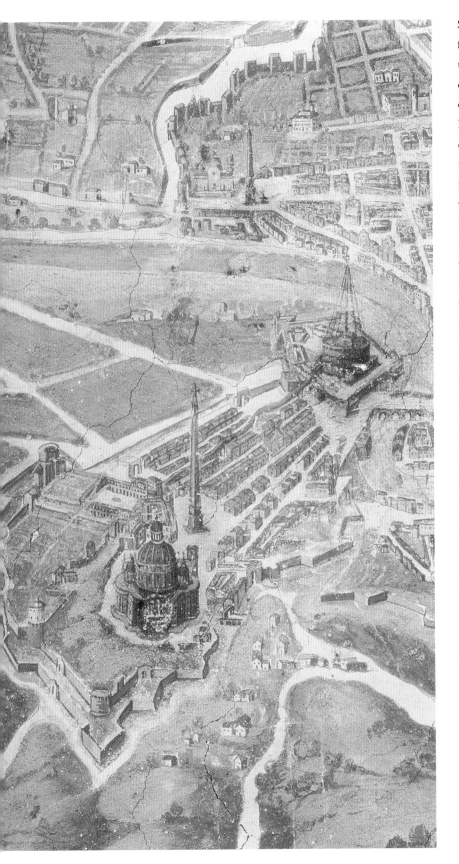

Sixtus also devoted money and energy to beautifying Rome. He instituted a major programme of urban renewal, brought a new water supply to the city, and rebuilt or remodelled more than a dozen churches and palaces. In this, he seems to have been motivated by impatience with inefficiency. If there was a problem, then solve it; if there was a job to be done, then do it. For example, St Peter's was still without the immense dome which Michelangelo had designed for it before his death in 1564. So at the end of 1588 the architect Giacomo della Porta and eight hundred workers began to labour day and night, and even on Sundays, to complete it. Sceptics said the work would take at least ten years; the last stone, inscribed with the Pope's name, was laid in position in May 1590. St John Lateran, the main papal residence until Nicholas V moved to the Vatican in the 15th century, had been neglected to such an extent that it was virtually uninhabitable. Soon after he became pope, Sixtus V ordered its demolition, even though parts of it dated from the sixth century. A new Lateran palace was finished four years later, in 1589. The Vatican's collection of books and manuscripts was inadequately housed; so a new library was built, again at breakneck speed.

Sixtus went to great lengths to improve communications around Rome. He banned overhanging wooden structures from the streets as a hindrance to traffic, and built a new aqueduct to bring water into the city. More than 120 streets were paved or repaved, and some 10 kilometres (6 miles) of entirely new roads were laid out, including a network of straight thoroughfares linking various focal points. The Strada Felice (now the Via Sistina) ran from Santa Croce in Gerusalemme in the south-east to Santa Maria Maggiore and on to Trinità dei Monti, a distance of 3 kilometres (1.8 miles); further avenues linked Santa Maria Maggiore with the Lateran Palace, and the Lateran with the Colosseum.

it stemmed from something more than mere philistinism. Whereas during the early Renaissance the Church, in common with humanist artists, had looked to classical Rome for inspiration and legitimization, Sixtus was concerned with the future of the Church rather than the past. As part of an overall effort to recreate Rome as the undisputed capital of Christendom, he used antiquity not to sanctify the Church, but to demonstrate the inadequacy of classical culture in comparison with the power of Christ as expressed by his vicar on earth. Imperial Rome was pagan Rome; far from being venerated, its architectural memorials had to be conquered and converted as ruthlessly as a heathen or a Protestant heretic.

In practice, this involved much more than destruction. Even if the city had consented to wholesale demolition – and it certainly would not – Sixtus V's programme of subordinating classical remains to Christian values was altogether more sophisticated. On one level, it meant employing religious imagery in place of traditional pagan icons; a typical example is the use of Moses striking the Rock, rather than the more conventional Neptune, to decorate a fountain. Elsewhere, however, Sixtus made a public display of the conquest of classical Rome. The removal of St Peter's obelisk to the piazza in front of his basilica – and

Only Sixtus's death prevented him from extending this network until all the major churches – and many of Rome's classical monuments – were linked by wide roads.

The Pope's attitude toward the architectural monuments of the past was unequivocal; he showed them no respect at all. So in spite of local protests, the remains of Septimus Severus's palace were demolished and their marble and travertine taken away to be reused on the Pope's new buildings. "Pagan" antique statues on the Capitol were removed. Even the Colosseum was to be converted into a wool factory, one of several measures designed to alleviate unemployment in the city. Work had already started on the project when Sixtus's death brought it to an abrupt halt.

The Pope's near-contempt for the buildings of antiquity that were still littered around the city was not all that uncommon. However, in his case

the substitution of a cross for the original mithraic golden ball – is just one instance. This process was repeated with three other obelisks, all of which were crowned with crosses and re-erected with great ceremony: one in the piazza in front of St John Lateran, another before Santa Maria Maggiore, and the third at the main entrance to the city. More public still was the treatment meted out to two of ancient Rome's greatest survivals. Trajan's Column, erected by Hadrian in the second century AD and covered with an exquisite spiral relief containing 2500 carved figures, was crowned with a bronze statue of St Peter; it was consecrated in a ceremony during which the Pope explained to the assembled crowd that such a monument could only be worthy to bear such a holy statue if it was cleansed of the pride and vanity which had produced it and rededicated in the cause of the Catholic Church.

Two years later the Column of Marcus Aurelius in the Piazza Colonna was topped with a statue of St Paul, and similarly rededicated. Antique bronzes were melted down to cast the figures.

Sixtus V was a sombre, frightening man, who managed to separate his personal inclination towards austerity from the splendours of his role. Much of the architecture of his pontificate has been dismissed as second-rate by art historians, who complain that he sacrificed the medium to the message and put speed of execution before quality. But his refusal to pay homage at the shrine of classicism, his determination to make architecture the slave of ideology, paved the way for the baroque of the 17th century – the most perfect architectural expression of an ideology ever seen. Without Sixtus V, there would have been no Bernini and no Wren. Without Sixtus V there would have been no Versailles.

ABOVE **The Sistine Hall in the Vatican (1587–9), built by Domenico Fontana. Murals glorify various events of Sixtus V's reign. The Pope was monastically austere and retiring by temperament, but well able to separate his personal life from the pomp and grandeur that he felt were due to his office.**

CHAPTER 4

EAST AND WEST

The 17th century was an uneven period for European court architecture. In the Low Countries, where the Calvinistic and democratically inclined citizens would not stand for princely displays of power, royal building projects tended to be fairly small-scale and restrained. Most of Germany was devastated by the Thirty Years War, which left its impoverished rulers in no position to embark on large-scale building projects. In Spain, secular architecture was overshadowed by the products of the Catholic Church – a fact which would probably have pleased Philip II, had he lived to see it. One also thinks primarily of the Church in connection with Italy's greatest baroque architects: Bernini and the Piazza of St Peter's, for example, or Borromini and San Carlo alle Quattro Fontane.

PREVIOUS PAGE **The Taj Mahal** on the banks of the Jumna river at Agra. Though it is famous as Shah Jahan's grand gesture of mourning for his dead wife, the mausoleum was also a statement of power.

RIGHT **A Moghul emperor** presides over his court. The long tradition of Eurocentrism in the West makes it too easy to ignore architectural and cultural developments in Asia and the Far East.

ABOVE **Louis XIV presides over a tournament in the courtyard of the Palace of the Tuileries in Paris. By the end of the 17th century every monarch in Europe envied his ability to orchestrate image-making set pieces like this.**

In England, the period was dominated by two court architects, Inigo Jones and Christopher Wren, who between them served under eight sovereigns from James I to George I. Sadly, most of those sovereigns were broke; and Wren's state apartments for William and Mary at Hampton Court Palace (1689–94) were the nearest any English monarch came to enjoying the axial planning and dynamic massing of palatial baroque.

It is the French court of Louis XIV at Versailles that shines like a beacon of arrogance and hauteur in a particularly arrogant and haughty age. Versailles is one of the greatest – if not the greatest – vision of single-minded, autocratic, absolutist architecture in the world. It eclipsed everything that came before, and set the standard for everything which followed – in western Europe, at least. But there is more to the world than western Europe. It might seem perverse to group together, as

this chapter does, the buildings of four such wildly different men as Christian IV of Denmark, Prince Toshihito of Japan, the Moghul Emperor Shah Jahan, and Louis XIV. Apart from the fact that they all held political power at some point during the 17th century, they have nothing in common. Christian was a Protestant and Louis a Catholic, Shah Jahan a Muslim and Toshihito a Buddhist. Louis was the most powerful monarch in Europe; Shah Jahan presided over a decline in Moghul fortunes in India; Christian was frankly a disaster as a king; and Toshihito rejected public life entirely to pursue his own super-refined private pleasures. No four people could be less similar. Yet they all shared a drive to express their personalities, their status, and their political aspirations in brick and stone. Compare and contrast them if you like; or if you prefer, just enjoy what follows as a celebration of diversity.

CHRISTIAN IV AND FREDERIKSBORG

In 1577 the Danish court astronomer Tycho Brahe predicted that the son just born to Frederick II of Denmark would be a "brave and skilful warrior" with "a good mind... and an interest in the arts and sciences." However, Prince Christian would also be "much disposed to high living [and] very fond of sensual pleasures." Tycho concluded by warning the baby: "You will yourself have brought on the sickness from which you will die, owing to exaggerated dissipation and too great indulgence in food and drink."

ABOVE **Christian IV (1577–1648), the "Builder King" of Denmark whose enthusiasm for architecture was equalled by his appetite for strong drink and sex, sat for this portrait by Pieter Isaacs in 1612.**

Tycho's prophecy was surprisingly accurate. Christian IV grew into a big, physical man with an impetuous nature which made him a good drinking companion but a bad statesman and a worse husband. A few days after marrying Anna Catherine of Brandenburg in November 1597, he took a mistress, who promptly presented him with the first of his many illegitimate offspring. Anna Catherine died in 1612, after bearing him seven children, and he took as his second wife the 17-year-old Countess Kirsten von Schleswig-Holstein, while continuing to run a stable of royal mistresses. Throughout his long reign he moved happily between the court and a flock of illegitimate families, the last of which belonged to Kirsten's maid.

Christian's devotion to drink was also legendary. He delighted in holding drinking contests with his courtiers – which he always won – and used to mark with a cross in his diary the occasions when he was put to bed drunk, adding a second cross for the nights when he could not stand, and a third when he was unconscious. In 1606, while he was on a state visit to England to see his sister Anne of Denmark and her husband James I, the British court's attempts to keep up with him ended in farce. After dinner a masque was put on for the King in which a lady of the court, representing the Queen of Sheba, offered him gifts of wine, cream, jellies, and cakes. But she tripped over the dais, tipped her gifts into his lap and fell on top of him. Christian tried to alleviate her embarrassment by dancing with her, but he was so drunk that he collapsed at her feet and had to be carried to bed, still covered in cream and jelly, while in the mean time three other players in the masque – Faith, Hope, and Charity – fluffed their lines and staggered downstairs, where they were later found "spewing in the lower hall."

Christian combined his Rabelaisian lifestyle with a determination to make his country a major military and economic force in Europe, although without much success. An expedition to Sri Lanka in 1618 – an attempt to emulate the Dutch and the English by establishing a trading post in the East Indies – came to nothing; and hoped-for trading links with Africa and China never materialized. Possessed of extraordinary personal courage in battle, Christian assumed command of the Protestant faction in the Thirty Years War in 1625, only for his forces to be routed by the Catholic League one year later. And when he led his fleet into battle against Sweden in 1644 at the age of 67, he lost an eye, an ear, and a large chunk of Danish territory as a result.

He was, however, a discerning and cultivated patron, and here he met with more success, amply fulfilling Tycho Brahe's prophecy that he would have a good mind and an interest in the arts and sciences. He took an enthusiastic interest in shipping and navigation, partly as a means of furthering his expansionist policies but also because, like Peter the Great, he simply liked sailing. He also encouraged the work of Dutch and German artists and craftsmen, and brought so many talented foreign musicians to the Danish court that by the early 17th century Copenhagen was hailed as the music capital of Europe.

But his greatest efforts were directed towards architecture. While he was still in his early 20s, the "Builder King" began to remodel the medieval stronghold of Koldinghus in Jutland, and he went on to initiate dozens of major projects. The most famous is the Copenhagen Bourse (1619–40), but there were also fortified towns, ports, and trading centres, all with names that proudly proclaimed their provenance – Christianopel, Christianstaad, Christianshavn, Christiania, Christianspriis, Christianssand. At Roskilde Cathedral, he added a new chapel in 1613, gave the elaborate reredos and the beautiful sandstone and alabaster pulpit, and

ABOVE **A view of Frederiksborg, Christian's most impressive building, painted by Ferdinand Richardt in 1848. Plans for the fortress-palace were drawn up in 1596 by the court architect Hans van Steenwinckel the Elder, although the King played an active personal role in its evolution over the next 30 years.**

replaced the existing stepped gables of the two western towers with the slender spires which are still the most memorable feature of the exterior. His role in these building works extended far beyond that of mere patron; he directed the workmen, sent plans and engravings for them to copy, and even negotiated contracts; and the presence in the royal library of books by Jacopo Vignola, Sebastiano Serlio, Vriedeman de Vries, and Jacques Androuet du Cerceau demonstrates his keen interest in architecture.

The Builder King's greatest work was the royal palace of Frederiksborg. When he came to power in 1596, he decided that the Danes needed a palace that would stand comparison with those of other European monarchs. Copenhagen Castle was too close to the commercial district and was in any case inconvenient and filled with government offices; other royal mansions were either little more than hunting lodges, or gloomy, heavily fortified castles, not at all in keeping with the sort of Renaissance princedom to which Christian aspired. The place which had the most potential was Frederiksborg, a country seat acquired by his father in 1560 at Hillerød, 25 kilometres (16 miles) north-west of Copenhagen. It stood on a group of three small islands in the north Zealand hunting country that Christian loved, and by the time of Frederick II's death in 1588 consisted of a stable block on the first island; a church, domestic offices, and the kitchens on the second; and the residential block on the third.

Plans for a large-scale remodelling of Frederiksborg began in 1596, and by 1601 they were well advanced. Frederick II's stables were left intact, but the mansion, the church, and the kitchens were demolished, and in 1602 work on new buildings began, continuing into the 1620s.

BELOW **The interior of the King's Winter Room at Frederiksborg. No expense was spared in the decoration of the palace.**

The middle island was given over to a Castellan's House and a Chancellery, which face each other across an open court with a large fountain designed by the Dutch sculptor Adrian de Vries between them. Beyond this entrance courtyard, and linked to it by a short bridge, is the palace itself, a U-shaped arrangement in red brick with stone dressings, consisting of three high ranges with a fourth, much lower and amounting to little more than a screen wall, connecting the arms of the U. The four-storey King's Wing, which housed Christian's apartments and was completed by about 1606, is in the centre, flanked by the Chapel Wing to the west and domestic offices to the east. The whole composition may owe something to the engravings of du Cerceau, but there is a lack of symmetry that would not have been tolerated further south in Europe at this date. A high bell-tower juts out unexpectedly from the courtyard facade of the Chapel Wing, for example, with no answering projection on the domestic block; and the chapel's gothic windows jar with the very classical pedimented windows of the other wings.

The interiors are marvellously rich and exuberant, and no expense was spared in their decoration. Most of the floors were of marble. Angels in the carved, moulded, and painted chapel vaulting looked down on a spectacular ebony, silver, and gilt altarpiece commissioned from the Mouridsens, a noted family of Hamburg goldsmiths. The 47 metre- (154 foot-) long hall above the chapel boasted tapestries depicting some of Christian's rather rare military victories, a ceiling painted with panels praising his encouragement of Danish crafts, and a chimneypiece covered with richly ornamented plates of solid silver.

Although Christian enjoyed the delights of Frederiksborg, his favourite residence was Rosenborg, a more modest palace just beyond the walls of Copenhagen, designed by the King in collaboration with Hans van Steenwinckel the Younger. It was begun in 1606 and extended at

least three times over the next 30 years, although it retains an air of compact simplicity that makes it one of Christian's most attractive buildings.

The King died in his bedroom at Rosenborg on 28 February 1648. The previous year his son and heir-apparent had drunk himself to death. Christian's attempts at territorial and economic expansion had resulted in the disastrous loss to Sweden of Danish possessions in the Baltic and near-bankruptcy at home. Even the silver panels on the great chimneypiece at Frederiksborg had had to be melted down for coinage. The grand ambitions with which his reign had started half a century before were unfulfilled – apart from the buildings. Perhaps that was enough.

ABOVE **Rosenborg was begun in 1606 and designed by Christian himself in collaboration with Hans van Steenwinckel the Younger. It was the King's favourite residence and he died there on 28 February 1648.**

Christian's devotion to drink was also legendary. He used to mark with a cross in his diary the occasions when he was put to bed drunk, adding a second cross for the nights when he could not stand, and a third when he was unconscious.

SHAH JAHAN AND THE TAJ MAHAL

A ruler who built the Taj Mahal or the Pearl Mosque in Agra, the marble pavilions of the Red Fort at Delhi, or the Hall of Public Audience at Agra Fort with its legendary Peacock Throne would deserve to go down in history as a truly great patron of architecture. Each of them could hold its own against anything produced on the Indian subcontinent. So when we realize that one man – Shah Jahan, "the Ruler of the World" – was responsible for all of them, respect is due.

ABOVE **Shah Jahan (1592–1666) and his favourite wife, Mumtaz Mahal. When she died in childbirth in 1631, "the world-discerning eye of the world-conquering King was flooded with tears."**

OPPOSITE **The Taj Mahal at Agra, the mausoleum of Mumtaz Mahal. Shah Jahan intended to build an identical mausoleum for himself in black marble and to link the two with a bridge. But the plan was abandoned and the Emperor was buried with his wife.**

When he succeeded his father Jahangir as Moghul emperor of India in February 1628, at the age of 36, Shah Jahan began to indulge a passion for architecture that dated back to his adolescent years at his father's court in Kashmir, perhaps even to childhood conversations with his grandfather Akbar, the builder of Fatehpur Sikri (see pp.56–9). He established his capital at Agra, where he immediately set about replacing Akbar's sandstone buildings with a palace of his own. The various elements were conventional enough, and differed little in their function from those of Akbar's time. There was a *diwan-i-am* (Hall of Public Audience) opening onto a great courtyard, where the people gathered each morning to present petitions or simply to watch the Emperor receiving dispatches from the provinces, dispensing justice, and making appointments. Behind this, across a formal square laid out with pools, channels, and fountains, was the *diwan-i-khas* (Hall of Private Audience), where Shah Jahan met daily with his close advisers to discuss more important matters

of government. A stair behind the *diwan-i-khas* led to the Emperor's private quarters in the Jasmine Tower and his private mosque, the Mina Masjid; and below them, to the south, was the *zenana* (women's quarters).

But if Shah Jahan's palace was laid out on orthodox lines, its architecture was immeasurably more sophisticated and opulent than that of his predecessors. Most obvious was his predilection for marble instead of the traditional red sandstone. It is in evidence everywhere at Agra, from the sublime simplicity of the Pearl Mosque to the north of the palace (which takes its name from its simple marble interior) to royal pavilions like the Khas Mahal and the delicately cusped arcades of the *diwan-i-am* itself. Carved and sculpted, inlaid with *pietra dura* work, raised on sandstone plinths, or topped with gilded domes and *chatris*, the marble pavilions of the Agra palace suggest that Shah Jahan was a ruler who was deliberately marking out his reign as different from – and greater than – those that came before; a ruler who understood the value of architectural display.

And so he did. While he was still remodelling the Agra Fort – as soon, in fact, as he came to the throne – Shah Jahan decided that the most public area of the palace, the *diwan-i-am*, should be given

"These lofty and substantial buildings... in accordance with the Arabic saying, "Verily our relics tell of us," speak with mute eloquence of His Majesty's God-given aspiration and sublime fortune – and... will serve as memorials of his abiding love of construction, ornamentation, and beauty." SHAIKH ABD AL-HAMID LAHORI

a focus, an architectural statement that would awe the assembled masses and impress upon visiting dignitaries the Emperor's immense wealth and power. So he commissioned a new throne for himself, one that would follow traditional Moghul lines – a cushioned seat shaded by a canopy – but would be so heavily stylized, so emblazoned with gems, that in the words of the court historian Nizam ud din Ahmad Bakshi, "majesty might shine with increased brilliancy". According to Nizam, "the outside of the canopy was to be of enamel work with occasional gems, the inside was to be set with rubies, garnets, and other jewels, and it was to be supported by twelve emerald columns. On the top of each pillar there were to be two peacocks thick set with gems, and between each two peacocks a tree set with rubies and diamonds, emeralds and pearls. The ascent was to consist of three steps set with jewels of fine water. This throne was completed in the course of seven years at a cost of 100 lacs of [i.e. 10 million] rupees."

In March 1635, at the auspicious vernal equinox, Shah Jahan occupied his new Peacock Throne in a grand audience in the *diwan-i-am*. For the remainder of his 30-year reign he led an increasingly sybaritic and sedentary life. His forebears had been military men, constantly on the move as they subdued rebellions and annexed territories; Shah Jahan now allowed his sons to lead the military campaigns which

were part of the inexorable Moghul southwards, and devoted more and more of his time to his jewels, his architecture, and the love of conspicuous display presaged by the Peacock Throne. He became heavily dependent upon a ceremonial lifestyle at court in which pleasure and ritual played equal parts. From dawn, when he showed himself to the people from the palace walls in the ceremony of the *jharoka-i-dharsan* while elephants were paraded in the space below to amuse him, to dusk, when he retired to bed while readers chosen for their agreeable voices read to him from behind a screen in his chamber, the Emperor's pursuit of pleasure was relentless. Even his daily council of state in the *diwan-i-khas* was regularly interrupted by a procession of subordinates bringing new works of art, jewels, even cheetahs and falcons, for his inspection.

In 1639, with many of the buildings at Agra still being planned or incomplete, the Emperor decreed that the court was to move to the traditional Indian capital of Delhi, where a new imperial city, Shahjahanabad, was to be built. The chronicler Inayat Khan describes how "throughout the imperial dominions, wherever artificers could be found, whether plain stone-cutters, ornamental sculptors, masons, or carpenters, by the mandate worthy of implicit obedience, they were all collected together." The complex was completed in nine years, and on 18 April 1648 Shah Jahan – complete with Peacock Throne – made his grand entrance into his new citadel.

As with Agra, the Red Fort at Delhi (named after its sandstone perimeter walls) was laid out as a series of courts, formal gardens, and white marble pavilions. There are many of the same features – the cusped arches, the swelling petalled domes, the extravagant *pietra dura* decoration – but if anything, the effect is even more opulent. Greatest of all the interiors is the *diwan-i-khas*, where the Emperor's glittering throne stood beneath a gilded ceiling, surrounded by marble

BELOW **A view into one of the marble courts in the palace at Agra. Shah Jahan demolished virtually all of the sandstone pavilions built here by his grandfather Akbar in the 16th century, replacing them with marble.**

walls and piers alive with painted and inlaid flowers and arabesques. Even today, 250 years after the Peacock Throne itself was carried off to Persia and broken up, the chamber remains a triumph; in Shah Jahan's time, when it was lit by scented candles and draped with precious silks and exotic carpets, the effect must have been breathtaking.

By the time that Shah Jahan moved his capital to Delhi, his most famous building project was already well under way. On 17 June 1631 his favourite wife, Mumtaz Mahal ("the Chosen of the Palace"), died giving birth to their 14th child. She was 28 years old. "The world-discerning eye of the world-conquering king was flooded with tears," and work began on her tomb, now known by a corruption of her name, the Taj Mahal.

Masons and carvers came from all over Asia to work on the tomb, which took 22 years to complete. The marble was quarried at Makrana, 320 kilometres (200 miles) west of Agra, while gems and semi-precious stones were imported from as far away as Egypt, Russia, and China. There has

been and still is a great deal of debate about exactly who was responsible for the design. The court histories, of course, give Shah Jahan himself a leading role in the creation of his major buildings, recording how he drew up the initial plans, made appropriate alterations to architects' drawings, and wrote down "his sacred judicious notes to serve as a guide for the building overseers and architects." Much of this may well be true; certainly it is more credible than the 18th- and 19th-century western tradition that the Taj Mahal was so beautiful that it must have been the work of a European. Persian sources give the credit to a Persian masterbuilder, Ustad Isa Afandi, about whom nothing else is known; while other contenders include Jahangir's chief architect, Mir Abd al-Karim, and Shah Jahan's minister of royal works, Makramat Khan, both of whom supervised the building work. The current favourite is the engineer, astronomer, mathematician, and architect Ustad Ahmad of Lahore, who worked on Shahjahanabad and whose son recorded that

"At the orders of the world-conquering king he constructed the edifice of the tomb of Mumtaz Mahal." The truth of the matter is probably that, like most Moghul buildings, the Taj Mahal was a collaborative effort involving a number of people, with Shah Jahan taking an important role, but as patron rather than designer.

The tomb must be one of the most photographed buildings in the world, and it is a measure of its greatness that familiarity breeds nothing but wonder. Standing at the northern end of a geometrically patterned garden about

"If there be a paradise on earth, it is here, it is here, it is here." INSCRIPTION ON A WALL AT THE RED FORT, SHAHJAHANABAD

300 metres (984 feet) square which is quartered by formal stone water-courses, and flanked by a mosque to the west and the mosque's *jawab* ("echo") to the east, it is raised on a high marble platform with tall, spiky minarets at each corner. The central dome rises to a height of 57 metres (187 feet), and is topped by a brass finial which adds another 17 metres (56 feet). Koranic inscriptions, flowers carved in low relief, and the most delicate *pietra dura* work cover almost every surface, and within the octagonal main chamber lie the bodies of Mumtaz Mahal and her husband (who was buried here in 1666), enclosed within filigree screens cut from solid slabs of marble.

Generations of European romantics have seen in the Taj Mahal a monumental expression of grief and conjugal devotion, "the ultimate expression of earthly love," in the words of one writer; as if such beauty must inevitably be the product of intense emotion. This underestimates the achievement of the armies of craftsmen who actually did the work, of course. It also conveniently ignores the fact that there was a well-established Moghul tradition of spectacular tomb-building – the Emperor Humayun's tomb in Delhi, for example, or that of Sher Shah in Sasaram. More importantly, it fails to take account of the idea that the Taj Mahal, like so many funerary monuments, is a more potent memorial to its builder than to his dead wife.

Apart from its artistic achievements – and partly because of the time and money that he poured into them – the King's reign was not particularly successful. In an attempt to match his huge expenditure, he relied on taxation rather than economic growth, and this, together with oppressive measures against Hindus and Christians and a series of disastrous military campaigns, tended to destabilize the Moghul Empire. Shah

LEFT **The *diwan-i-am* (Hall of Public Audience) at Shahjahanabad. The Emperor moved to the capital in April 1648, when for the first time he occupied his splendid new Peacock Throne in a grand audience in the *diwan-i-am*.**

Jahan was also cursed with the Moghul emperors' problem of power-hungry offspring, and when he fell ill in late 1657, no fewer than four of his sons began a battle for the throne. Aurangzeb, the third son, won, and in 1658 he declared himself emperor, while his father was kept under house arrest in Agra Fort until his death eight years later.

Shah Jahan may not have done too well as a leader of men. But as a patron and connoisseur, India had never seen his like, nor would again. In the words of his court historian, Shaikh Abd al-Hamid Lahori, "These lofty and substantial buildings... in accordance with the Arabic saying, "Verily our relics tell of us," speak with mute eloquence of His Majesty's God-given aspiration and sublime fortune – and for ages to come will serve as memorials of his abiding love of construction, ornamentation, and beauty." Less wordy but infinitely more eloquent is an inscription in the *diwan-i-khas* at the Red Fort in Shahjahanabad: "If there be a Paradise on earth, it is here, it is here, it is here."

BELOW **A detail of the Taj Mahal. Many Western observers have seen the mausoleum as the quintessential architectural expression of lost love, ignoring the fact that within weeks of Mumtaz Mahal's death, her grieving husband had found consolation in the arms of his young daughter.**

TOSHIHITO AND THE KATSURA IMPERIAL VILLA

In the summer of 1625 the abbot of the Zen temple of Nanzen-ji at Kyoto was invited to Katsura, a summer villa which had recently been built on the outskirts of Kyoto by the Emperor of Japan's uncle, Prince Hachijo Toshihito. The abbot repaid the Prince's hospitality with a hymn of praise to his new mansion: "In this glorious age, multitudes of workers and hundreds of craftsmen were assembled, brooks dug, hills moulded, flowered palaces built, and jewelled pavilions erected."

BELOW **The pavilions and gardens of the Katsura Detached Palace, created in the 1620s by Prince Hachijo Toshihito (1579–1629), the uncle of Emperor GoMizuno-o of Japan and an ardent aesthete.**

Katsura was built – and perhaps even designed – by Prince Toshihito (1579–1629), the younger brother of the Emperor Go-yozei, and extended or completed by his son, Prince Noritada (d. 1662). As a child, Toshihito had been adopted by Toyotomi Hideyoshi, the great general who managed to unify Japan after generations of internecine fighting. Then, as now, the role of the Japanese emperor was largely ceremonial, and in terms of political power this early connection

with Hideyoshi promised much more than Toshihito's blood-relationship with Go-yozei. However, the boy's prospects came to an abrupt end when the general fathered a son of his own, and in compensation, Toshihito was created a prince in 1590. By the time he was in his early thirties he had become personal adviser to his nephew GoMizuno-o, who came to the throne in 1611. He was an urbane and accomplished diplomat who spent much of the 1610s mediating between the imperial court and the Tokugawa shoguns, who had seized power after Hideyoshi's death in 1598 and who were in effect the military dictators of Japan. His greatest success came in 1620, when after protracted negotiations, GoMizuno-o married Tokugawa Kazuko, a daughter of Shogun Hidetada; and with the bride's entry into court he all but abandoned politics to devote himself to literature, the arts, and the summer villa at Katsura which he began to build in that year as a retreat from worldly affairs.

The residential complex stands within a compound roughly 150 by 165 metres (492 by 541 feet), and consists of three asymmetrical and interconnected single-storey blocks which look out onto an irregular-shaped pool. In traditional Japanese style, they are all constructed of wooden

posts and lintels, so the walls are not load-bearing and can contain wide door- and window-openings to give good views of the gardens. The floors are raised a metre (3 feet) or more above the ground, partly because the area was subject to periodic flooding from the Katsura river which flows past less than 100 metres (305 feet) away, but also, again, to make the best of the views.

The first block, and the one which visiting courtiers would enter after their palanquins had been set down at the door, is the Old Shoin, which the Prince used for informal entertaining. Inside there are a series of plainly decorated rooms partitioned by wide *fusuma*, sliding paper-covered screens. None of them is particularly large; using the standard Japanese modular measurement, the *tatami* (a rectangular rush mat just

under 2 metres by 1/6.5 feet by 3), even the biggest chamber in the complex, an L-shaped main reception area, is only a 15-mat room with maximum dimensions of 7 metres by 5 (23 feet by 16). There is nevertheless a tremendous sense of space, not least because the chamber opens out onto a verandah, which in turn gives onto a bamboo platform, where Toshihito and his guests could gather to admire the moon and its reflection in the pool below. Moon-watching was a favourite pastime among the cultured nobility; long before the Prince began his villa, Katsura was already famous in literature for "its beautiful moon," and it is quite possible that this was a decisive factor in Toshihito's choice of site. It may well be that the unusual alignment of the residential buildings, which face 19 degrees south-east rather

ABOVE **The main residential block of the palace. In contrast to the usual Japanese practice of lining up on an exact north-south or east-west axis, Katsura's alignment is slightly askew, so that Toshihito could obtain the best possible views of the harvest moon.**

LOUIS XIV AND VERSAILLES

In August 1661 the 23-year-old Louis XIV attended a grand fête held by his finance minister, Nicolas Fouquet, at Vaux-le-Vicomte, just south-east of Paris. The King was impressed both by the scale of the celebrations – 6000 guests, a huge firework display, a _comédie-ballet_ by Molière, "statues" and "trees" that came to life and spoke – and by the grandeur of Fouquet's new chateau, with its formal avenues and vistas, its airy, elegant interiors, and elaborate allegorical murals.

ABOVE **Louis XIV (1638–1715, seated on the right) and members of the royal family depicted as the gods on Mount Olympus by Jean Nacret in 1670. The painting hung in the antechamber to the King's bedroom at Versailles, as a reminder to courtiers that their master was the most powerful man in Europe.**

Louis was less impressed by the fact that Fouquet had redirected a hefty slice of public funds towards the building of Vaux-le-Vicomte. In fact the young King was so angry that his mother had to restrain him from having his finance minister arrested in the middle of the party. But she persuaded him that such conduct would be unseemly with the advice "Not in his own house; not at an entertainment held in your honour", and Louis agreed to wait. Three weeks later Fouquet was arrested for misappropriation; he died in prison in 1680.

Louis gained an enormous amount from Fouquet: his furniture, paintings, and tapestries; his artists and craftsmen; and his self-confessed ambition to build a chateau which would "leave some traces of the status I had enjoyed." The major focus of Louis' own architectural ambition was Versailles, a hunting lodge which his father had built in 1624 in the forests 25 kilometres (16 miles) west of Paris. It had been extensively remodelled by Philibert Le Roy between 1631 and 1634, but when Louis took personal control of affairs of state on the death of Cardinal Mazarin in 1661, the lodge was still a modest building – three ranges of red brick with stone dressings and slate roofs, grouped around a central courtyard, with little square pavilions at the corners. His initial impulse was merely to renovate the chateau as a pleasant rural retreat; he added gilded balconies to the roof, built a new self-contained kitchen block and an orangery (which he stocked with orange trees taken from Vaux-le-Vicomte), and extended the gardens in a series of large formal parterres. The work was more or less finished by the early summer of 1664, when a grand fête was held to celebrate its completion – another lesson in conspicuous consumption that Louis had learned from Fouquet.

As the 1660s wore on and the King's gardener, André Le Nôtre, continued to extend the gardens, the chateau was dwarfed by an immense western axis with parterres, temples, and grottos, a grand canal, and a host of other waterworks. (There were about 1400 fountains in the grounds by the time Le Nôtre had finished.) After toying with the idea of sweeping away Louis XIII's chateau and starting all over again on a scale to match the grandeur of the gardens, the King decided in 1669 to retain the original building while surrounding it with state apartments for the royal family to the north, south, and west – a scheme that Louis' chief minister, Jean-Baptiste Colbert, referred to as the "Enveloppe." Louis Le

Vau, the designer of Fouquet's Vaux-le-Vicomte, was chief architect, and although he died in 1670, the work continued until around 1678 – only for the King to decide that the new building was still too small. He was moving towards the idea of making Versailles the official seat of the French government, a step which would involve accommodation and offices for literally thousands of courtiers, officials, and servants. The Enveloppe was altered and vastly extended, this time with Jules Hardouin-Mansart as supervising architect. With Charles Le Brun (who had also worked on Vaux-le-Vicomte) in charge of the interior decoration, Mansart produced a scheme for new state and private apartments, including the magnificent

BELOW **By the time this bird's-eye view was painted in 1668, Louis had made some minor alterations to his father's hunting lodge at Versailles, but most of his energies had been spent creating the spectacular formal gardens. The following year, the King began remodelling on a grand scale, surrounding the existing chteau with state apartments.**

ABOVE **The Marble Court, showing the (much-altered) chateau of Louis XIII at the heart of Versailles. Louis XIV's apartments were on the first floor; the room where he held daily meetings of his Council of State is on the right, and the three windows in the centre light the bedchamber where he died on 1 September 1715.**

OPPOSITE **The Hall of Mirrors, which runs almost the entire length of the west front of the palace, was where Louis XIV received visiting ambassadors. Le Brun's ceiling murals depict military and economic triumphs from the King's reign.**

Hall of Mirrors which, at 73 metres (210 feet) long, runs almost the entire length of the west front, and two immense ranges of government offices and lodgings to the north and south of the main block. Across the palace square, facing the entrance facade (which still had at its core the old chateau of Louis XIII), there were two immense stable blocks, one for the King's hunters and the other for his coach-horses. So large and well-appointed were they that the Elector of Hanover was prompted to complain that Louis' horses were better housed than he was.

Long before the King's death in 1715, Versailles had become the archetypal vision of power. After Louis formally announced on 6 May 1682 that it would henceforth be the seat of government, making a triumphal entry shortly afterwards into what was still a virtual building site, the rest of Europe quickly became aware of how it enhanced the King's prestige. Charles XI and Charles XII of Sweden kept diplomats in France between 1693 and 1718 solely to report back to the royal architect on the latest trends. Schönbrunn, the great house outside Vienna designed for the Holy Roman Emperor Leopold

III in 1696, was inspired by the Sun King's palace. Even William of Orange, who rejected Louis' expansionism, his Catholicism, and his concept of absolute monarchy, attempted to rival Versailles, first at Het Loo in the Netherlands and then, after his accession to the British throne in 1689, at Hampton Court. There is a certain irony in the story of his representative on a visit to Versailles in 1697 who, when asked whether William's palace had anything to compare with what he saw, replied self-righteously that "the monuments of my master's actions are to be seen everywhere but in his own house." That may have been true, but considering the money and effort poured into reconstructing Hampton Court on the French model, it was not for want of trying.

Versailles became – and remained – the standard by which all other royal building projects were judged, just as Rome was the empire by which all other empires were measured. Het Loo was called "the Dutch Versailles"; Peter the Great's early 18th-century palace of Peterhof, built after a visit to see the real thing, was dubbed "the Russian Versailles"; even as late as the 1870s Ludwig II spent a fortune attempting to build a Bavarian Versailles at Herrenchiemsee.

Part of the attraction was the realization that Versailles was a tremendously effective announcement of the power that a single man wielded. In the 1660s Colbert had told Louis that "with the exception of brilliant military actions, nothing speaks so eloquently of the grandeur and cleverness of princes than buildings." Of course the King knew that already; since the Renaissance, everybody knew it. But until now, nobody had conceived the idea of a head of state building as a personal statement, on such a grandiose scale. Although to talk of a personal statement is perhaps misleading; the palace is inextricably linked with Louis' public image, but that public image was actually indistinguishable from his private image – he was a walking, talking

ABOVE **The Salon of War is completely dominated by Coysevox's bas-relief of Louis as a Roman general on horseback, trampling his enemies underfoot. The Hall of Mirrors can be seen through the archway.**

metaphor for absolute monarchy, whose every action was performed in front of, and for the benefit of, an audience. At Versailles the court watched him eat; the court watched him dress and undress. The only times he was not under public scrutiny were during his dutiful fortnightly visits to his wife's bed, or his less dutiful but more frequent visits to his mistress's.

The cult of personality was reinforced at Versailles with a thoroughness and wit that hadn't been seen in Europe since the Roman emperors. On the day that Louis was born, 5 September 1638, the French Mint had struck a commemorative coin with the inscription *Orbus Solis Gallici*

("Thus rises the Sun of France"). For the rest of his life, the sun was Louis' special symbol and the sun-god, Apollo, his allegorical alter-ego. At Versailles the presence and power of the Sun-King was expressed in a variety of different forms. Jean-Baptiste Tuby created the famous statue of the sun-god Apollo emerging from the sea on his chariot, for the Basin of Apollo at the eastern end of the Grand Canal (see opposite). Closer to the palace is a fountain by the Marsy brothers which depicts the legend of Latona, the mother of Apollo, who was mocked by peasants as she tried to drink at a Lycian lake, and responded by calling on Zeus to turn her tormentors into frogs –

a witty but unquestionable warning to the King's subjects. And also in the grounds, to the north-east of the palace, stood the Grotto of Thetis, a monumental pavilion housing a life-sized statue by François Girardon of Apollo at rest. The Grotto provided courtiers and foreign visitors to Versailles with a statement of the palace's function; like the sun-god himself, the Sun-King came here to rest and put aside his cares; but, as Madeleine de Scudéry pointed out in 1668, the King was always ready to return promptly to the task of ruling France, "with the same fervour as that with which the sun begins to illumine the world when he rises from the waters where he has rested himself."

The cult was continued with renewed vigour in the palace itself, but with a more serious tone that went hand-in-hand with Versailles' developing role as the seat of government rather than the royal retreat suggested by the Grotto of Thetis. Charles Le Brun's ceiling-panels in the Hall of Mirrors show Louis' recent military conquests in the Netherlands; the most spectacular, "The Crossing of the Rhine," depicts the King as Apollo in his chariot, accompanied by Hercules, who is obligingly clubbing the prostrate Rhine-god. In the Salon of War (see opposite), pride of place was given to a bas-relief by Coysevox of Louis as a Roman general on horseback, trampling his enemies underfoot. And the throne room beyond, where Louis sat on a silver throne beneath a canopy of state, was the Salon d'Apollo; ostensibly named for Charles de la Fosse's painted ceiling of the sun-god in his chariot, it was obviously intended to suggest to visiting dignitaries that they were, metaphorically at least, in the presence of a god-like monarch.

The palace is filled with tangible reminders of Louis XIV's pronouncement that "L'état c'est moi" ("I am the state"); a painting of the gods on Mount Olympus by Jean Nacret in the antechamber to the King's bedroom gives them the faces of

"Versailles alone suffices to secure forever to France the glory it has at present, in surpassing all other kingdoms in the science of building: and it is beholden for this high esteem to the grandeur and magnificence of Louis the Great." GUIDE TO VERSAILLES (1681)

Louis and his family (see p.104); busts and portraits of the King adorn almost every room. An early guide to the palace, written in 1681, announces that Versailles was not only a homage to Louis XIV, it was a product of his greatness: "Italy must now yield to France the prize and garland which it has borne hitherto from all the nations of the earth, in regard to the excellency of architecture, the beauty of the carving, the magnificence of painting... Versailles alone suffices to secure forever to France the glory it has at present, in surpassing all other kingdoms in the science of building: and it is beholden for this high esteem to the grandeur and magnificence of Louis the Great."

The message was clear; the Sun-King's rays illuminated French arts. In the gardens and state-rooms of Versailles, where Apollo in his chariot rode across the sky to define a nation and an era, the architecture of power was changed forever.

BELOW **The Basin of Apollo, with Jean-Baptiste Tuby's statue of the sun-god emerging from the sea. From the day of his birth, when the French mint struck a commemorative coin with the inscription "Thus rises the Sun of France," Louis XIV used Apollo as his allegorical alter-ego.**

PALACES OF POWER

Nero's legendary Golden House had an impressive portico 1.5 kilometres long (1 mile wide) and an atrium big enough to hold a statue of the Emperor 36 metres (118 feet) high. Wild animals roamed beside a vast artificial lake in the grounds, and the vaulted interiors were decorated with gold, gems, ivory, and mother-of-pearl. Panels in the ceilings could swivel to shower Nero and his guests with flower-petals; hidden pipes sprayed them with perfume; and the circular banqueting hall revolved day and night, like the heavens. Yet far from being excited at the prospect of this hedonistic urban paradise, Nero merely said that, at last, he would be housed like a human being.

PREVIOUS PAGE **Ludwig II of Bavaria floats with the swans in his shell-shaped boat, in the specially constructed Venus Grotto at Linderhof, from an illustration of 1886 by Robert Assmus.**

LEFT **Domestic bliss at Windsor Castle depicted by the artist Siegfried Bendixen; many European monarchs of the 19th century had to embrace solid, respectable middle-class values, as Victoria and Albert did so wholeheartedly, or face losing their palaces and their thrones.**

OPPOSITE **Prague Castle, the last refuge of the Austrian Emperor Ferdinand I. He was only one of a number of heads of state who were forced from power in 1848, as revolution swept across Europe.**

There were plenty of European monarchs in the later 18th and 19th centuries who looked back wistfully to the time when a ruler could regard a stupendous palace like the Golden House as no more than his due. They may not have seen Nero as a great role model; apart from his appetite for treachery and debauchery (an appetite which many of them shared, but which now had to be pursued in private), he had a megalomaniacal streak as wide as the Tiber and an unutterably vulgar taste in interior decoration. But the power to command buildings on such a grand scale was something most of them could only do in their dreams.

Between the accession of Catherine the Great in 1762 and the death of Ludwig II of Bavaria in 1886 the power of Western monarchs declined steadily. The two most dramatic 18th-century rejections of monarchism, the American Declaration of Independence and the French Revolution, were followed in the first half of the 19th century by risings against established rule in Spain, France, Italy, Serbia, and Greece. They culminated in the wave of revolutions of 1848, which affected almost every country in Europe. Insurrection in Vienna led to the abdication of the Austrian Emperor, the intellectually disadvantaged (and now monarchically disadvantaged) Ferdinand I, who retired to the royal castle at Prague (see right). In France, the February Revolution forced Louis Philippe to flee to England, using the unimaginative pseudonym of "Mr Smith." Pope Pius IX was ejected from Rome, where a republic was proclaimed. And in Bavaria, Ludwig I abdicated in favour of his son Maximilian (although this was the result of his affair with the Irish dancer Lola Montez, rather than radical revolt).

As this chapter shows, the architectural consequences varied according to circumstance. In the 1780s Catherine the Great, who hardly felt threatened by her serfs, adopted the classical trappings of the Enlightenment as a fashion statement; a few years later Jefferson and Washington sought to appropriate classicism for their more earnest republican ends. In Britain, George IV clashed head-on with his government during the 1820s over his right to build his own Golden House at Buckingham Palace. Fortunately for Europe – although not for fans of camp architecture – few rulers went as far as Ludwig II, whose quest for a lost absolutist state led to bizarre fantasies like Neuschwanstein. All these heads of state built palaces of power. But even as they built, that power was changing hands.

CATHERINE THE GREAT AND TSARSKOYE SELO

When Catherine the Great became Empress of all the Russias in July 1762, after her supporters had poisoned and strangled her unappealing husband Peter III, Tsarskoye Selo was already the imperial family's favourite summer residence. In 1708 Peter the Great had presented the estate, just south of St Petersburg, to his wife, Catherine I. She commissioned J. Braunstein to design the Palace of the Sixteen Rich Rooms, later known as the Catherine Palace after its first owner.

ABOVE **Catherine the Great (1729–96) walking one of her English greyhounds in the gardens at Tsarskoye Selo, painted by V. Borovikovsky. The column in the background commemorates a Russian naval victory over the Turks.**

The complex was vastly enlarged for the Empress Elizabeth (reigned 1741–62), first by the court architect Savva Chevakinsky in 1745, and then by the French-born Bartolomeo Rastrelli, the leading exponent of St Petersburg baroque. Rastrelli's facade is a glorious synthesis of the heavy, theatrical forms of European baroque with the even heavier, even more theatrical colour schemes of Russian tradition. White columns and gilded and bronzed details were offset against turquoise walls, and the whole composition was capped with a silver-painted roof (see right).

However, when Catherine the Great came to the throne, Russian baroque fell from grace as dramatically as her husband. Catherine was not merely an admirer of European culture; she was a European, the daughter of a German prince. She read Rousseau and Racine, debated with Diderot and corresponded with Voltaire. The first words of the *Instruction*, the philosophical statement of government which she issued in 1767, were "Russia is a European country."

In 1779 Catherine wrote to a friend that she had acquired the services of "a Mr Cameron, Scottish by nationality, Jacobite by persuasion, a superb draughtsman, nourished on antiquities and known for a book he has written on ancient baths. We are creating together a terraced garden with baths below and a gallery above." The reference was to Charles Cameron (c.1743–1812), who was invited to Russia on the strength of his *Baths of the Romans Explained and Illustrated*, and who was to transform the Catherine Palace into one of the neoclassical wonders of Europe. Cameron was the son of a Hackney builder with an unsuccessful career as a surveyor behind him. During the 1760s he spent some years in Rome researching his book and claiming close (and wholly fictitious) links with the Stuarts in a vain attempt to obtain commissions from Jacobite émigrés who lived in the city. But against all the odds, Catherine's invitation to Tsarskoye Selo – and her determined encouragement of Cameron's far-from-obvious talent – brought out an unexpected genius.

Cameron's first project, a two-storey bath house just south of the palace, was an immediate success with the Russian court. When it was completed in 1792, Catherine could progress from a canopied cold bath of white marble, with a bronze gilded seat beneath the water, via a warm bath to the hot room, where steam was created by pouring water onto a little mountain of 250 red-hot cannon balls. Suitably invigorated, she could then relax on an antique couch – presumably with a friend, judging by the pictures of famous couples (Cupid and Psyche, Venus and Adonis, Endymion and Diana) with which Cameron decorated the hangings around the couch. The sybaritic splendours of the baths were echoed on the floor above, a series of small cabinets or closets surrounding a central hall. Known as the Agate Rooms (see p.117), these chambers were covered with allegorical paintings, mythological panels, and medallions in plaster, and details picked out in bronze and gilt over expanses of veined marble, crimson agate, green jasper, and mountain crystal.

In 1784, Catherine commissioned Cameron to design a two-storey gallery connected to the Agate Rooms and her private lodgings. Another deliberate evocation of antiquity – "Here idols were preserved, and altars smoked with sacrifices," wrote the 18th-century poet Gavril Derzhavin – the Cameron Gallery was a place where the Empress could admire the views over her gardens while simultaneously soaking up the inspirational atmosphere of the ancient past that the Enlightenment had taught her to prize. It was filled with busts of ancient philosophers, gods, and emperors – Socrates and Plato, Apollo and Minerva, Julius Caesar and Vespasian. She

BELOW **The east facade of the Catherine Palace at Tsarskoye Selo, designed for the Empress Elizabeth by Bartolomeo Rastrelli and built between 1749 and 1752. The beginning of Catherine the Great's reign marked a move away from such baroque melodrama towards a purer and more fashionable neoclassicism.**

ABOVE **Stucco decoration in Charles Cameron's Green Dining Room (early 1780s), part of the suite of state apartments designed for Catherine's son and heir, Grand Duke Paul Petrovich.**

RIGHT **The Hermitage (1744–56), by Rastrelli, is set on a star-shaped piece of land surrounded by a moat. It is one of a number of pavilions, temples and follies that were built in the gardens at Tsarskoye Selo.**

OPPOSITE **The central hall of the Agate Rooms on the first floor of Cameron's bath-house. The opulence of its decoration made the architect's name famous throughout Russia; the poet Derzhavin called it "a chamber worthy of Olympus."**

admitted only two contemporary heroes to the pantheon: the poet Mikhail Lomonosov, who had recently died; and the British politician Charles James Fox, who was very much alive. Catherine's particular fondness for British culture seems to have deepened during the last years of her life. As well as admiring Fox and giving Cameron free reign to create his own brand of neoclassicism at Tsarskoye Selo, she brought over British masons and plasterers. Her head gardener was John Bush, who until 1771 ran a nursery garden in Hackney. Her park was laid out in the English style, heavily influenced by landscapes of association like Stowe. ("I adore English gardens," she said to Voltaire.) There was a Temple of Memory, a Ruined Tower commemorating a victory over the Turks in 1771, a Triumphal Arch – even a pets' mausoleum where she buried two much-loved greyhounds given to her by her English physician, Thomas Dimsdale.

Between 1780 and 1788 the interiors of the Catherine Palace itself were remodelled, again to the designs of Charles Cameron. Two state apartments, one for the Empress and another for her son, the Grand Duke Paul, were created to either side of the central hall and grand staircase. Each had its own reception halls and dining rooms as well as bedchambers, cabinets, and private lodgings; both were virtually destroyed by the retreating German army at the end of World War II. Thankfully, many of the rooms in the Grand Duke's apartment have now been restored, including Cameron's masterly Green Dining Room, a light and airy Adamesque composition in pale green, white, and pink in which stately plaster figures look down on the diners, surrounded by putti, fantastic etiolated columns, and writhing foliage (see left). Much work remains to be done in Catherine's own wing; the Arabesque Hall, the Chinese Hall, the Domed Dining Room, and the rest of the apartments are known only from black-and-white photographs, 19th-century paintings and drawings, and written descriptions, such as the Empress's own account of her Silver Study, "a little room made of solid silver embossed with a pattern of red leaves... very pleasant."

"Very pleasant" is something of an understatement. By the time of Catherine's death in 1796, her summer residence was one of the most famous palaces in Europe. Even patronizing Western visitors could not help but marvel at the magnificence of the Agate Rooms, the sheer good taste of the Cameron Gallery, the park that outdid the English in its Englishness. As a symbol of the Russian Enlightenment, Tsarskoye Selo had not only matched its western European rivals; it had outdone them.

Secretar
elling.
remains
1787, a
particul
facade
Paris; o
single
above a
the idea

For
accomn
ern fac
rooms

ABOVE **Jefferson's bedroom, with its bed ingeniously, if rather curiously, set into an open alcove. He soon found the arrangement much too draughty, and closed in one side of the alcove with paper screens.**

Well, no, it doesn't, actually. The confident handling of spaces that one finds in the work of European neoclassicists; the high standard of craftsmanship; above all, the ability to adapt classical motifs and turn them into something new and exciting: these things are missing in Jefferson's house. There is an undeniably provincial air about Monticello which, in spite of La Rochefoucauld's optimistic remarks, smacks of too much book-learning. Elements were drawn from Palladio, of course, as they were in the work of many contemporary European architects; they range from internal decorative mouldings to the

"Having expanded his architectural studies beyond books to the architectural models of Europe, the new Monticello will deserve to be ranked with the most pleasant mansions in France and England." LA ROCHEFOUCAULD

stepped central dome, which derives from Palladio's elevation of the Temple of Vesta in the *Quattro Libri*. But there is a host of other quotations, some from French works like Fréart de Chambray's *Parallèle de l'Architecture* (1650), many from the English neo-Palladians. Jefferson's designs for garden pavilions rely heavily on *Designs of Inigo Jones* (1727) by William Kent and Lord Burlington, and James Gibbs' *Book of Architecture* (1728). Gibbs was also the source of the bull's-eye windows around the dome's drum; the octagonal parlour at the heart of Monticello was copied either from the same architect or from *Select Architecture* (1755), a popular pattern-book by the English Palladian Robert Morris.

There is nothing wrong with architectural quotations. But the whole needs to be greater than the sum of its recycled parts, and at Monticello, the various elements do not always sit together too happily. For instance, some of the bedrooms on the upper floor are squeezed in above the suite of ground-floor living rooms that flank the hall and parlour, and lit by windows placed abruptly on top of the living-room windows. They are another borrowing, perhaps, from the town-houses which Jefferson saw during his stay in Paris – but Monticello is not a town-house, and the sense of space given by the panoramic mountain-top views is strangely at odds with the cramped effect of the tightly tiered windows.

Internally, the greatest solecism is the treatment of the area beneath the dome, which in Palladio's Villa Rotonda is carried up through the full height of the house to create a great room, an internal focus of which the dome is a natural external expression. Jefferson had no use for such a grand and imposing space, and besides, it smacked of an aristocratic pomp that was at odds with his radical egalitarianism. So he gave the parlour a flat ceiling and hid the dome away in the attics, producing a disturbing sense of disappointment and confusion after the expectations aroused by the exterior.

Neither the errors nor the over-reliance on pattern-books can be dismissed as ignorance or lack of talent. In addition to all his other accomplishments, Thomas Jefferson was a tremendously gifted architect. The Capitol in Richmond, which is based on the Maison Carrée in Nîmes, was a brilliantly imaginative scheme, the first real neoclassical building in America and one of the first in the world to emphasize the sanctity of public institutions by literally building a temple to democracy. The "academical village" he designed for the University of Virginia at Charlottesville (see right), with its Pantheonesque rotunda (where, incidentally, he did appreciate the value of the dome as an internal space) is a tour de force. And Jefferson's contribution to the building of the Federal City (see pp.122–5) defined the nature of American public architecture.

Monticello's problem is that it is not public architecture. The constant rebuilding, the awkward tensions between different elements, the references to European pattern-books: all betray a lack of confidence. They suggest Jefferson was unsure as to what values private architecture should express in the new republic. Classicism was admirably suited for the evocation of pride in nationhood and the dignity of civic institutions – it legitimized, it sanctified. Create those qualities in a private home and you are in danger of finding yourself sitting in a palace; from there it is a short step to deciding that while all men are created equal, some are more equal than others.

BELOW **The Rotunda at the University of Virginia, Charlottesville. With public buildings, such as those of his "academical village" at Charlottesville, Jefferson was much more confident in his handling of a classical vocabulary than he was with a private residence such as Monticello.**

GEORGE WASHINGTON AND THE FEDERAL CITY

In the inaugural address that George Washington gave at New York City Hall in April 1789, America's first president set out the high stakes that the nation was playing for – nothing less than "the preservation of the sacred fire of liberty, and the destiny of the Republican model of Government." He might have added that the success of America's great experiment would depend on the establishment of federal institutions of government; and those institutions required a permanent capital – a federal city.

ABOVE **Charles Wilson Peale's portrait of George Washington (1732–99). Although he worked hard to push the scheme for a federal capital through Congress, America's first president had only a superficial knowledge of architecture, and was content to leave most of the details to Jefferson.**

The job of designing the Federal City was entrusted to Pierre Charles L'Enfant, a French war artist and architect who had fought for America during the Revolutionary War. In March 1791 Washington commissioned L'Enfant to survey the chosen site, on the banks of the Potomac river, and to establish the positions of public buildings. The Frenchman proposed that the new capital should consist of a regular grid-pattern aligned on the points of the compass, but broken up by tree-lined "grand transverse avenues" 50 metres (164 feet) wide, which opened into squares and piazzas with "grand fountains" and "grand edifices." (Grandeur was clearly uppermost in L'Enfant's thinking.) The centre-piece was a triangle formed by three points: a presidential palace; an equestrian statue of George Washington roughly on the site of the present Washington Monument; and a congress house raised up on Jenkins Hill, which L'Enfant described as "a pedestal waiting for a monument." Statue and congress house were linked by a wide promenade (now the Mall); and the congress house was linked to the palace by the hypotenuse of the triangle, the present Pennsylvania Avenue. The arrangement of radial vistas is heavily influenced by the layout of

Versailles, and even more by Christopher Wren's unexecuted but widely published designs for a baroque London, done in the weeks following the Great Fire of 1666.

The two buildings which provided the raison d'être of the new city were the presidential palace and the congress house. L'Enfant's plan was approved in the late summer of 1791, and in September Secretary of State Thomas Jefferson and the three Commissioners appointed by the President to oversee the project met at Georgetown and agreed that the city should be named after Washington. But Jefferson, ever the guardian of liberty and enemy of the cult of personality, took steps to ensure that the Federal City should not become a Versailles-like homage to a new ruler. The presidential palace became the more egalitarian "President's House," and the congress building was to be called "the Capitol," after the Capitoline Hill in Rome, the political centre of the model for all republics. The style chosen for the public buildings was uncompromisingly classical; Jenkins Hill became Capitoline Hill and – just in case the cultural references had been missed – the name of a little inlet below the site of the federal buildings was changed from Goose Creek to the Tiber.

At this point the dream of a new Rome began to turn sour. The works were to be financed by the sale of 10,000 building plots, but at a public auction in October 1791, attended by the President and Secretary of State Jefferson, only 35 plots were sold – and four of those were bought by the Commissioners in an attempt to stimulate interest. The plain fact was that no-one wanted to live in a city which was still little more than a swampy morass in the middle of nowhere.

Things were complicated further by the autocratic attitude of the city's architect. The intention was that L'Enfant would design both the Capitol and the President's House, with Jefferson providing advice. But the architect refused to show the Commissioners his plans for the Capitol; nor would he allow them the use of his city map for the auction of lots. He ordered the demolition of new houses which encroached on his planned public avenues, including one being built by Daniel Carroll, the nephew of one of the Commissioners. And when Washington stepped in to mediate, L'Enfant responded with a categorical refusal to submit to their authority. At the end of February 1792 Washington reluctantly ordered Jefferson to inform L'Enfant that "your services must be at an end."

With no architect to design the vital government buildings, no money to build them and no-one willing to settle in the Federal City, the vision

ABOVE **A 19th-century view of the President's House, designed by James Hoban in 1792, and later altered by both Hoban and Benjamin Latrobe. John Adams was the first president to live here. When he moved in, in 1800, the building was still incomplete, and there were no water closets.**

"In fancy now beneath the twilight gloom,
Come, let me lead thee o'er this "second Rome"…
This embryo capital, where Fancy sees
Squares in morasses, obelisks in trees" POEM BY THOMAS MOORE (1804)

LUDWIG II AND NEUSCHWANSTEIN

"There on the mountain top stands the citadel of the gods," sings Wotan in _Das Rheingold_. "In a dream I conceived it; my will called it into being." For Ludwig II, the ill-starred King of Bavaria, the misty Wagnerian world of gods and heroes was infinitely more appealing than the real world of diplomacy, political manoeuvres, and affairs of state, and during his short life he conceived and called into being not one but three glittering Valhallas in which he could hide away from reality.

ABOVE **Ludwig II of Bavaria (1845–86) as Grand Master of the Knights of St George, painted shortly before his death. The artist, Gabriel Schachinger, has evoked to perfection the qualities of inner strength and regal authority that were so disastrously lacking in his subject in real life.**

The first and most famous was Schloss Neuschwanstein, a collection of Romanesque-style towers and turrets on a mountain top in the Bavarian Alps about 130 kilometres (80 miles) south-west of Munich. Then came the exotic baroque villa of Linderhof, near Oberammergau; and finally Herrenchiemsee, a monumental new Versailles on an island in the Chiemsee to the east of the capital. "Oh!" wrote Ludwig, "it is essential to create such paradises, such poetical sanctuaries where one can forget for a while the dreadful age in which we live."

The idea for Schloss Neuschwanstein dates from 1867, when the 21-year-old King, a passionate Wagnerite and the composer's most generous patron, made a pilgrimage to the Wartburg, the castle in Thuringia which had been the setting for _Tannhäuser_. Later that summer he also visited Pierrefonds, the 14th-century castle outside Paris which Viollet-le-Duc had recently restored for Napoleon III. By May 1868 he was writing to Wagner with a plan for a fortress of his own: "I propose to rebuild the ancient castle ruins of Vorderhohenschwangau, near the Pöllat Falls, in the genuine style of the old German knights' castles..." It was to be a temple to his "godlike friend," he said, with reminiscences of

Tannhäuser and _Lohengrin_; on a more prosaic level, it would also enable him to spend time in his beloved mountains while avoiding the attentions of his mother, who passed her summers at the royal residence of Hohenschwangau further down the mountain.

Work began on Neuschwanstein that summer, when the ruins of the medieval castle which had occupied the site were demolished and a level platform was blasted out of the mountain. The man responsible for the initial design was the court architect Edward Riedel, who came up with a fairly conventional late gothic scheme; but this was neither picturesque enough nor dramatic enough for Ludwig, and although Riedel remained architect in charge until 1874 (when he was replaced by George Dollmann), the King relied heavily on the drawings and sketches of Christian Jank, a Munich set-designer who had contributed to various Wagner operas staged in the city by royal command during the late 1860s. (Between 1865 and 1870 _Tristan und Isolde, Die Meistersinger, Das Rheingold_ and _Die Walküre_ were all premiered in Munich, and there were gala performances of _Lohengrin_ and _Tannhäuser_.) Instead of being "in the genuine style of the old German knights' castles," Neuschwanstein

became a homage in stone to a decidedly theatrical medievalism. Romanesque was used instead of gothic, a reference to the early 13th-century setting for *Tannhäuser*. The huge Minstrel's Hall was Jank's own vision of the Hall of Song at the Wartburg castle from *Tannhäuser*, and everywhere in the turreted five-storeyed Palas or keep which houses the royal apartments, murals depict the great heroes and heroines of High German Romance. Tristan woos Isolde in the King's Bedroom, Tannhäuser whiles away his time with Venus in the study; and in the other reception rooms Parsifal proves himself worthy of the Holy Grail and Lohengrin defends Elsa in single com-

bat. Only in the Throne Room, not decorated until 1881, does the theme falter temporarily. In an allusion to Ludwig's wistful faith in absolute monarchy and the divine right of kings, a Byzantine Christ in his glory is flanked by the Six Christian Kings, European monarchs ranging from Kasimir, King of Hungary, to Edward the Confessor of England, all of whom were canonized for their faith. Beneath them is the plinth where Ludwig was to sit on his throne, sanctified by God and accompanied by saintly kings (see p.132). The throne of gold and ivory was never put in place – a poignant reminder of just how out of time his ideas were.

ABOVE **Schloss Neuschwanstein was begun in 1868 as a mountain-top retreat in the "genuine style of the old German knights' castles." The theatrical fortress in the Bavarian Alps was still incomplete in June 1886, when a delegation of doctors and courtiers arrived to arrest the King and have him certified as insane.**

BELOW **Eduard Ille's 1867 design for the Throne Room at Neuschwanstein, originally intended as a Hall of the Grail for the premiere of Parsifal, is highly coloured, in both senses of the phrase. Ludwig, who was going through a Byzantine phase at the time, instructed Ille to base his design on Hagia Sophia in Constantinople.**

The notion of a European monarch building a mock-medieval castle was not particularly unusual in the 19th century. George IV had done it at Windsor; so had Napoleon III at Pierrefonds. In the 1850s Victoria and Albert had built themselves a Scotch Baronial retreat at Balmoral Castle in the Highlands, and Ludwig's own father, Maximillian II, had "restored" the family's summer residence of Hohenschwangau in the gothic style in the 1830s. But Ludwig's vision of the past was at once more vivid and less healthy than theirs. He did not simply seek a romantic setting in which to carry out the business of state or take holidays from the cares of kingship; he wanted to be Lohengrin, to act out increasingly weird fantasies which became a substitute for real life.

At Linderhof, the second of Ludwig's major building works, he turned to another of his pet obsessions – the Bourbons. A visit to France in 1867 had fuelled his belief in an almost mystical link between himself and the French kings of the later 17th and 18th centuries, a belief which stemmed from the simple fact that Louis XVI of France had been his grandfather's godfather. He read every book about life at the court of Versailles that he could lay his hands on; he ordered his dramatists to write plays about the period for him; and, about the time that Neuschwanstein was begun, he resolved to convert the small hunting-lodge of Linderhof in the Graswang valley near Oberammergau into a full-size replica of Versailles – a project which he code-named "Meicost-Ettal," an anagram of Louis XIV's "L'état c'est moi."

By 1869, when George Dollmann's designs for Linderhof were finally approved, the scale of the project had been considerably curtailed, and instead of Versailles, Dollmann created a sort of Petit Trianon, a compact pavilion in which a baroque facade conceals some astonishingly rich rococo interiors in gilt, stucco, and marble, all intended to conjure up the great days of the Bourbon court of the *ancien régime* (see the illustration of the King's Bedroom, opposite). Like the Munich stage-sets on which many of them are based, they are interpretations of an era rather than slavish architectural copies, evocations rather than replicas; but the world they evoke and interpret is constantly reinforced. There are portraits of Madame Dubarry and other members of the Bourbon court, paintings on porcelain of Louis XV at Versailles, of Louis XVI's coronation at Rheims – and on the terrace, which looks out over delightful French formal gardens laid out in 1877 by Ludwig's landscape gardener, Karl von Effner, a bust of Marie-Antoinette before which the King would pause each day to doff his hat, bow, and caress her cheek.

ABOVE **The King's Bedroom at Linderhof. Ludwig was obsessively interested in the absolute monarchs of 18th-century France, and used to order costumes to be sent from the Court Theatre in Munich so that he could play at being Louis XV.**

Ludwig's postponed Meicost-Ettal finally came to fruition in 1878 when work began on the lake-island palace of Herrenchiemsee in the south-east of Bavaria. The most ambitious of all his building schemes, it was never completed, but even in its unfinished state it is a breathtaking piece of creative fancy. Behind an entrance facade – which in typically Ludwigian fashion sought to improve on reality by interpeting what Versailles might have looked like if it had all been built by Louis XIV instead of incorporating Louis XIII's earlier chateau – lie the Galerie des Glaces, the Chambre de Parade – even a grand Ambassadors' Staircase, known only from engravings since the original at Versailles had been destroyed in 1752.

In the Venus Grotto at Linderhof, Ludwig could rock gently across an underground lake in a shell-shaped boat, while swans glided by and an arrangement of dynamos, arc lamps, and coloured glass disks produced a spectacular lightshow in blues and vivid pinks.

These were not rooms of state in any ordinary sense. Ludwig had his own bedroom, for example, preferring to keep the spectacular Chambre de Parade as a shrine to the Sun-King, and in any case, he only stayed at the house for one ten-day period in September 1885. As historians have pointed out, Herrenchiemsee was conceived from the outset as a monument to the absolute power that Ludwig yearned for but could never hope to achieve in a late 19th-century constitutional monarchy. It was a homage to Bourbon power, just as Neuschwanstein was a homage to Wagnerian legend.

By the time work started on Herrenchiemsee, the King's eccentric behaviour was beginning to cause his ministers concern. During the early 1870s he had begun to withdraw from public life, refusing to attend court dinners or meet with officials, sleeping by day and only rising at dusk, and reconciling his love of the theatre with his distaste for public appearances by ordering that his favourite plays, operas, and ballets should be performed at the Residenz Theatre in Munich for him alone, with no other audience present. (This obsession with privacy also showed itself in Ludwig's penchant for dining rooms with "magic tables" which could be lowered through the floor to a servery and raised again stocked with food, obviating the need to have even servants present while he ate.) He also began a more sinister journey into a twilight world where his buildings were backdrops against which he could act out the fantasy of the moment. At Neuschwanstein, he might dress up as the swan-knight Lohengrin; at Linderhof he would order costumes to be sent from the wardrobe at the Court Theatre in Munich so that he could play at being Louis XV. Schloss Schachen, a hunting chalet on the road to Linderhof, was decked out as an eastern pavilion where Ludwig would lie on cushions, dressed as a Turkish sultan, sipping coffee, and smoking a hookah, while young soldiers danced naked before him. No doubt he amused himself in the same way at Linderhof, in the Moorish Kiosk and Moroccan House which he had erected in the

> **"I propose to rebuild the ancient castle ruins of Vorderhohenschwangau, near the Pöllat Falls, in the genuine style of the old German knights' castles, and I must tell you how excited I am at the idea of living there..."** LUDWIG OF BAVARIA

grounds there (see opposite). When he tired of that game, he would pass the time in his Hundinghütte, a rustic hall built by Dollmann in 1876 around an ancient tree in the beechwoods near Linderhof, and based on Jank's designs for the first act of the Munich premiere of *Die Walküre*. (The tree should, of course, have been a sacred ash, so the plans stipulate that the trunk of the beech must be "covered with the bark of an ash.") Here he would loll on animal skins, reading from the sagas, drinking horns of mead with his

current favourite and imagining himself a warrior back in the world of Siegfried and Brünnhilde.

The most awesome of the buildings in the grounds at Linderhof, and in many ways the epitome of Ludwig's alarming retreat from reality, is the Venus Grotto, modelled on the cave beneath the Venusberg in *Tannhäuser* with a dash of the famous Blue Grotto at Capri thrown in. (The King dispatched one of his equerries to Capri to memorize the precise shade of blue, so that it could be reproduced accurately at Linderhof. Then he sent him back again to make sure he had it right.) In this artificial cave of canvas, cast iron, and cement, he could rock gently across an underground lake in a shell-shaped boat or sit on his shell-shaped throne, while swans glided by and 24 dynamos, 24 arc lamps, and an arrangement of coloured glass disks produced a spectacularly bizarre lightshow in blues and vivid pinks (for illustration see pp.110–11).

By 1886 Ludwig's ministers had decided he was mad. Certainly mental instability ran in the family: there was porphyria on his mother's side; his father's sister suffered from the persistent delusion that she had swallowed a glass piano; and the behaviour of his younger brother Otto was so outré and unpredictable – he used to bark like a dog, make faces, and shout obscenities in public – that in the 1870s Ludwig reluctantly agreed that he should be locked away. The King's own demons were more private, and thus ultimately less embarrassing; but his persistent refusal to concern himself with state affairs (and, one suspects, the presence of an endless procession of actors, soldiers, grooms, and other "unsuitable" male lovers) eventually led to a coup. The bewildered would-be absolutist monarch was arrested at Neuschwanstein on the night of 12 June 1886, certified as insane, and taken to Schloss Berg, another royal castle about 16 kilometres (10 miles) south of Munich. The following evening he went for a walk in the grounds, accompanied

by his psychiatrist, Bernhard von Gudden. The bodies of both men were found floating in the lake a few hours later.

No-one has satisfactorily explained Ludwig's death, although plenty of theories have been put forward – murder, suicide, even a heart attack brought on by the exertion of drowning Gudden. In their different ways, his buildings are just as problematic as his end. They suggest a king who – almost uniquely – was not concerned to create monuments to posterity or political statements for his subjects; a ruler who would rather live in a world of his own devising than rule in one he could not control. The games he played with architecture, the dreams of different realities in which he was Wagnerian hero or eastern potentate or elegant French autocrat, were just that – games and dreams. Even the absolutist fantasies have no real ideological substance, no serious political programme behind them. His buildings may have been visions of power, but it was a power that he longed for, yet never possessed.

ABOVE **The Moorish Kiosk in the grounds of Linderhof, one of several exotic lodges where Ludwig dressed as a sultan and smoked a hookah while young soldiers danced naked before him. The interior contained a specially built Peacock Throne.**

CHAPTER 6

THE GREAT DICTATORS

It is a paradox that one of the biggest problems in exploring the connection between architecture and ideology is that of separating the two – or to be more precise, of unravelling how far our response to a building or a style is coloured by what we think of the ideology of its builder, or know of the circumstances behind its creation. This is brought sharply into focus when it comes to the buildings of undemocratic, tyrannical, or morally corrupt political systems. The cynic may say that every political system is either undemocratic, tyrannical, or morally corrupt (or all three); but some are less equal than others. For example, we view the austere and unimaginative cityscapes of Romania or Albania with complacency. After all, weren't the Stalinist regimes that produced them austere and unimaginative?

PREVIOUS PAGE **The All-Union Agricultural Exhibition in Moscow, 1 May, 1940. The vast exhibition complex measured 136 hectares (336 acres) and boasted 230 pavilions.**

BELOW **A dance to the music of time? This stiff and rather mannered sculptural group outside the Theatre of Art in Pyongyang, North Korea, suggests that autocratic ideologies necessarily produce bad art. Unfortunately, things are seldom as straightforward as that.**

The colossal Kumsusan Memorial Palace in Pyongyang (opposite), with its carved slogans and giant statues, is just as paternalistic and oppressive as the man it commemorates, North Korea's leader Kim Il Sung. Of course, Jean-Bedel Bokassa's absurdly lavish palace in the Central African Republic is bad architecture – after all, he ate babies didn't he?

It is hard to be objective, and when it comes to the architecture of dictatorship, perhaps we should not even try. A dispassionate and apolitical discussion of, say, Albert Speer's designs for Hitler's Berlin seems about as appropriate as assessing the formal architectural qualities of Dachau. Like a concentration camp, the meaning that we attribute to a grandiose public building or a triumphal avenue or a whole city is deeply rooted in the circumstances of its production, its cultural context. And the imposition of a personal set of cultural values on a society is surely one of the defining characteristics of a dictatorship. Fascist architecture is faulty architecture, not because of what it is, but because of what it represents.

At least, that is what we would like to think. However, and perhaps regrettably, questionable or even downright evil political systems do not invariably produce bad or bland buildings. We only need to look to the less recent past for confirmation of that fact. The atrocities perpetrated by Kubilai Khan or Akbar were as barbarous as those of Stalin or Hitler; but because they happened so long ago, they don't seem quite so real, or quite so awful. The moral relativism that always operates in history means that long-dead tyrants somehow don't merit the condemnation we reserve for a Pol Pot or a Pinochet. In any case, their choices were limited – and perhaps this is key – by the age they lived in; it would be impossible to imagine a situation in which Kubilai Khan or Akbar suddenly called for free and fair elections. Time has long since washed away the blood from the buildings that were and still are an expression of their tyranny and oppression.

The five very different autocrats who figure in this chapter – Peter the Great, Napoleon III, Mussolini, Hitler, and Stalin – are linked by the fact that they all used architecture as a weapon in a battle for social and cultural control. They may not share the same circle in Hell and, as we shall see, they met with varying degrees of success. Yet some of the buildings they produced are quite beautiful – and our problem is to reconcile that beauty with the deeply flawed visions that produced it.

LEFT **Lenin is winched off his pedestal in Vilnius, Lithuania, in 1991, as the USSR falls apart. Most 20th-century dictatorships have used art to promote personality cults.**

BELOW **This 1939 issue of *Die Woche* (The Week) compares Bismarck's Germany (a scraggy heraldic eagle) with Hitler's Third Reich (a pure, clean-lined, monumental structure).**

PETER THE GREAT
AND ST PETERSBURG

"Paradise." That was Peter the Great's favourite term for St Petersburg, his favourite creation. To the Tsar, the city that rose out of the marshy delta at the mouth of the River Neva was a thing of joy, "like a child that is growing into beauty." Others were less enthusiastic. The nobles who were ordered to build residences in the new metropolis – and to live in them, rather than in Moscow – detested the mosquito-ridden climate, the frequent floods, the scarcity of provisions.

RIGHT **Peter the Great (1672–1725), by Jean-Marc Nattier. The Tsar's passion for all things European, which expressed itself in the architecture of St Petersburg, was acquired during a Grand Tour in the 1690s – the first time a Russian monarch had left the country for 600 years.**

OPPOSITE **The baroque spire of Domenico Trezzini's Cathedral of the Peter and Paul Fortress in St Petersburg (1712–33). The Swiss-born Trezzini spent most of his life designing buildings in the new city, and its architectural character is largely due to him.**

Foreign diplomats, forced to move to the city after it was designated the capital of Russia in 1712, dismissed its "bastard architecture" and joked that ruins make themselves in other places, but that they were built in St Petersburg. The general population was convinced that the whole project was the work of the Devil, and told each other stories of how Satan drove through the city streets in a carriage by night. Small wonder that the Tsar's court jester, allowed by custom to say to

Peter's face what others dared not, described the city as "On one side the sea, on the other sorrow, on the third moss, on the fourth a sigh."

Peter's "paradise" had its roots in Russian attempts to gain access to the Baltic coast. In 1702 Russian forces captured the Swedish fortress of Nöteborg, on an island just at the point where the Neva flowed out of Lake Ladoga to the sea. The following May, Peter's troops took Nienschanz, a second Swedish fortress which commanded the mouth of the river where it flowed into the Gulf of Finland. These two acquisitions formed the basis for the new city.

But the Tsar's ambitions extended far beyond the acquisition of a Baltic port. Between March 1697 and August 1698 he had made a Grand Tour of Europe – the first Russian prince to venture beyond his country's borders since the 11th century. He was so enthusiastic about what he saw that he returned to Russia fired with the desire to transform his country into a truly European state. "Why have we alone degenerate and rude souls? Why should we alone be left out as unworthy?" he asked. His subjects soon found that Europeanization was more than just an abstract notion. The day after the Tsar's arrival back in Moscow, nobles who had assembled to

greet him were horrified when he produced a pair of shears and cut off their beards, traditional symbols of religious orthodoxy. From now on, everyone was to be clean-shaven, like Europeans. And there was more: "For the glory and beautification of the State," announced a decree of 1700, men and women were to wear European dress. A simplified "civic alphabet" was introduced. The old Russian calendar (which began on 1 September 5508 BC, the date when the world was created) was brought into line with Europe. And as Peter's reign wore on, the trading posts and military installations that made up the first St Petersburg grew to be the public embodiment of Russia's drive to create a modern state.

An obvious first step towards creating a distinctively European city was the employment of European designers. During his tour of 1697–8, the Tsar had attempted to speed up the introduction of modern technology into Russia by recruiting upwards of 600 foreign experts – doctors, engineers, naval officers, and civil engineers. The process was repeated during the 1700s and 1710s with the importation of large numbers of architects and craftsmen. Chief among them was the Swiss-born Domenico Trezzini, who arrived in Petersburg soon after the fall of Nienschanz, and remained there until his death in 1734. Trezzini was the moving force behind much of the city's architecture. He supervised the conscript workforce, set up studios to train a new generation of Russian architects in the use of the classical orders, and designed a series of major buildings himself. They included the Tsar's Summer Palace on the banks of the Neva (1710–14), one of the first stone structures to be put up in the city; the baroque Cathedral of St Peter and St Paul (1712–33; see left); and the Twelve Colleges on Vasilevsky Island at the mouth of the Neva, a complex of administrative and government offices begun in 1722. Trezzini also played an important part in the design of St Petersburg's suburbs.

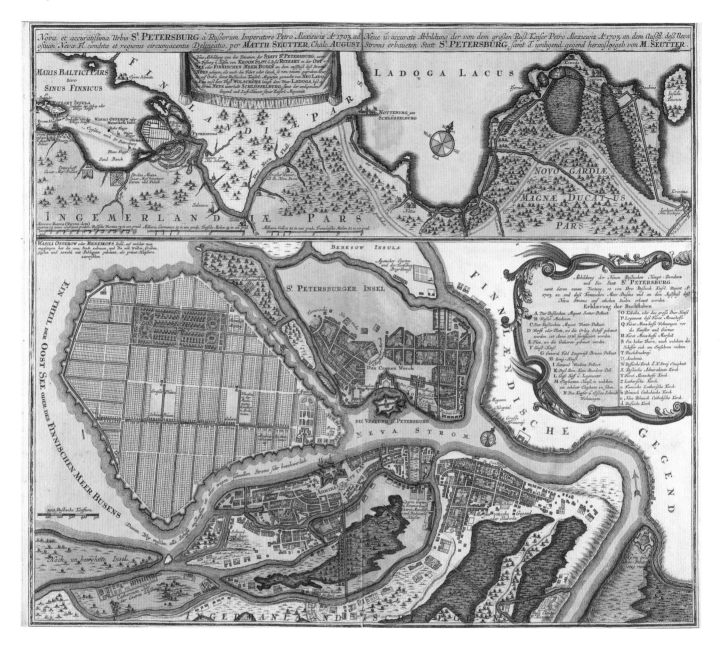

ABOVE **A 1728 map of St Petersburg. The Peter and Paul Fortress, the first building to be put up after the Russians occupied the area in 1703, is on the tiny island in the centre of the main picture. Vasilevsky Island, which Peter decreed would be the centre of the city, is on the left.**

Acting on Peter's instructions, he drew up model plans for villas, complete with six authorized variants for entrance gates and five for flanking pavilions. Anyone building on the city outskirts had to follow these plans.

Peter sent young Russian architects off on study trips to Holland and Italy, so that they could see at first hand exactly what it was that he sought to create in St Petersburg. But to begin with, at least, it was foreign architects who had the greatest impact on the development of the city, and a

steady stream of them soon followed Trezzini, making the long journey to St Petersburg from all over Europe. The German Georg-Iohann Mattarnovy designed a modest Winter Palace on the Neva for the Tsar in 1716, and the rather less modest Kunstkamera ("cabinet of art") on Vasilevsky Island two years later. Ostensibly a library and museum of natural science, the Kunstkamera definitely tended towards the unnatural. Like a Renaissance prince, Peter gathered together a huge collection of curiosities,

The Senate, the court, and government officials were commanded to relocate to St Petersburg from Moscow. Once there, they had to conform to decrees that regulated everything from the building materials they used for their houses to the size and shape of their chimneys.

from Siamese twins and a two-headed calf to the alarmingly large penis that once belonged to a member of his guard.

A flood of decrees and edicts fell on the hapless population, many of whom were only there in the first place because the Tsar had ordered their presence. In 1709 there were well over 10,000 conscript labourers in the city; by 1716 this figure had risen to 32,000. But Peter did not want a new capital populated only by labourers. He moved the Admiralty shipyards there in 1706, followed by senior members of his court two years later. When a fire destroyed a large area of Moscow, 5,000 families were forbidden to rebuild their houses and ordered to settle in St Petersburg instead. In 1712 he decided that the city, still little more than a collection of temporary wooden shacks and fortifications, must formally become the capital of Russia, and the following year the Senate, the remainder of the court, and hundreds of government officials were commanded to relocate from Moscow. Once there, they had to conform to decrees which

regulated everything from the building materials they used for their houses to the size and shape of their chimneys. If they failed to follow the officially sanctioned model plans for their houses, those houses could be pulled down. When Peter decided that Vasilevsky Island should be the new centre of the city, in spite of the fact that there were no permanent bridges connecting it to the mainland, he simply told everyone who had just built their model houses on the banks of the Neva that they must move again. "And if someone even after this announcement will not take these places and build their houses according to the decree, they will be severely punished."

Incredibly, Peter succeeded. By the time of his death in 1725, St Petersburg had become "a wonder of the world," in the words of the Hanoverian diplomat Friedrich Weber. When Catherine the Great came to the throne in 1762, the new city was already a cosmopolitan centre of culture, with a population of more than 100,000, thriving English, French, German, and Italian quarters, an academy of painting, sculpture, and architecture, ballet schools, opera, theatre. Tyranny and oppression are not supposed to lead to lasting success, yet in the case of St Petersburg they did. The Tsar's child may have lost its innocence as it grew into beauty. But for all his faults, Peter did manage to produce a paradise of sorts.

BELOW **After a visit to Versailles in 1717, Peter decided he would like something similar, and commissioned the Frenchman Jean-Baptiste Alexandre Leblond to design Peterhof on the shores of the Gulf of Finland. Its fountains, cascades, and canals duly earned the palace the title of the "Russian Versailles."**

NAPOLEON III
AND **PARIS**

Second Empire Paris is a byword for urban planning as social control. Its new boulevards were reputedly laid out with the purpose of putting an end to half a century of popular unrest. They were long and straight, so that government forces could direct artillery fire against rebel positions. They were wide, so insurgents would find them difficult to barricade. And they were deliberately driven through centres of working-class resistance, so that troops could move quickly to break up rioters.

ABOVE **The Emperor Napoleon III (1808–73), seen here in a portrait by Hippolyte Flandrin, was one of the first rulers to see urban planning as a means of social control.**

When Louis Napoleon was appointed President of the Second Republic in the aftermath of the bloody street-fighting of 1848, the capital of France was crying out for modernization. A policy of discouraging building outside the city limits had resulted in a population of well over one million being crammed into a relatively small area, forced to contend with winding, muddy alleys, open sewers and, especially at the eastern end of the city, a squalid labyrinth of overcrowded tenements. Even outside the slums, traffic regularly ground to a halt in the narrow streets, many of them scarcely wide enough for two wagons to pass. The water supply was woefully inadequate – only 20 per cent of houses had piped water, and hardly any had running water on the upper floors. In any case, there can have been little incentive to drink it; much of the supply was pumped direct from the Seine, at points downstream from the main sewage outlets.

Napoleon did little to improve the capital during his four-year term as president, largely because the Prefect of the Seine, Jean-Jacques Berger, opposed his plans. But as soon as he assumed power as emperor in December 1852, he replaced Berger with Georges Haussmann, a career civil servant with a track record as a strong supporter of Louis Napoleon. "Broadshouldered, bull-necked, full of audacity and cunning" and imbued with "a sort of cynical brutality," according to the duc de Persigny, the Minister of the Interior, Haussmann was just the man to push through radical change. On the day his new Prefect took his oath of office – 29 June 1853 – Napoleon III presented Haussmann with his personal scheme to transform the capital, and over the next two decades Haussmann almost single-handedly ensured that it was put into practice. He met daily with the Emperor and answered only to him. He ignored objections from the city authorities. And by raising loans, issuing bonds, and engaging in creative accounting, he managed to raise the enormous sums required to compensate landowners and pay contractors – 2.5 billion francs in total.

The most famous elements of Napoleon's scheme are the boulevards. The rue de Rivoli, which had been begun by Napoleon I, was extended to create a major east-west avenue. A corresponding north-south thoroughfare (now the boulevards de Strasbourg, de Sébastopol, du Palais, and Saint-Michel) was pushed through to the east of the Louvre, cutting through densely populated areas to cross the rue de Rivoli and

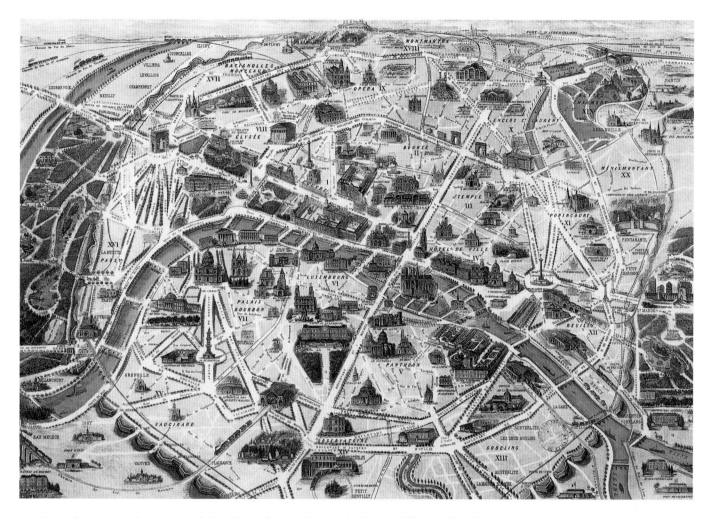

continue down over the river and the Ile de la Cité. Other streets were extended, straightened, or widened – or often, all three – both to facilitate movement within the city and to provide access to outlying areas that the government wanted to develop. Including the widening and reconstruction of 53 kilometres (33 miles) of existing streets, some 145 kilometres (90 miles) of new streets were built in Paris under Haussmann's direction; over 644 kilometres (400 miles) of pavement were laid and around 50,000 trees were planted. Yet the boulevards formed only one part of the development programme. There were also new schools, churches, and hospitals, and more than 100,000 new houses. Flagship projects included the Opera House, a new central market, the rebuilding of the city's main hospital, and exten-

sions to the Louvre. The facades of houses erected by private contractors had to conform to plans set down by the city authorities.

Aqueducts and pumping stations were built to bring clean water into the city, and Haussmann completely overhauled the inadequate sewerage system, installing 418 kilometres (260 miles) of sewers that became the envy of Europe. Three new parks and more than twenty landscaped squares were created in Paris itself, and Napoleon transferred the old state forests of the Bois de Boulogne in the west and the Bois de Vincennes in the east to the city as public parks.

ABOVE **Second Empire Paris, Napoleon's dream made real by Georges Haussmann. The map shows the wide, straight boulevards that were cut through the once densely packed streets in an effort to relieve traffic and, more importantly, to discourage civil disobedience.**

"Sir, it was said of Augustus that he found Rome brick and left it marble. May it be said of you that you found Paris stinking and left it sweet." SOCIAL REFORMER EDWIN CHADWICK TO NAPOLEON III

ABOVE **An assault on the barricades of Faubourg Saint-Antoine during the rising of June 1848. The memory of scenes such as this – where narrow streets and loose paving stones made barricade-building relatively easy – had a powerful effect on the planning of the new Paris.**

poverty. The little squares that were scattered around the city must have been small comfort for their occupants.

At a deeper level, many of Napoleon's new works were designed to emphasize his authority as emperor. His first major projects, the extension of the rue de Rivoli and the building of the Central Markets, had both been proposed by Napoleon I, but had stalled under successive republican and monarchist governments. In fulfilling his uncle's wishes, Napoleon III was both demonstrating to the nation that, unlike republics and monarchies, emperors got things done, and affirming the direct line between his own administration and the First Empire.

The maintenance of power and the suppression of dissent also played a vital part, however. Haussmann grasped the opportunities that the new works offered for political cleansing, saying that "the destruction of the old quarters removes a refuge for the rioters." It would be an oversimplification to say that the redevelopment sprang directly from a desire to strangle working-class opposition, but wherever the chance arose to outflank traditional centres of insurgency or to sweep away their memorials, it was seized. For example, the ostensible reason for extending the rue de Turbigo from the place du Château d'Eau (now the place de la République) down to the new Central Markets was to relieve congestion around the market halls; but it is no coincidence that it also meant the demolition of an important socialist stronghold around the Conservatoire des Arts et Métiers – and the destruction of the rue Transnonain, the scene of a massacre of republicans in 1834. There were sound practical reasons for Haussmann's decision in the 1860s to do away with the sandstone blocks used to surface Paris streets – they broke down under the wear and tear from hooves and carriage wheels. But they could be, and often had been, used as missiles on the barricades, something that would be

Disentangling Napoleon III's motives for reconstructing the capital is no easy matter. No doubt he saw improving the lot of Parisians as a good in itself, although with hindsight we can see that his concern scarcely stretched beyond the bourgeoisie who formed the backbone of his political support. They were handsomely compensated for the demolition of their houses and the relocation of their businesses; they could afford to subscribe to the issues of city bonds that helped to finance the work; they could drive out for an afternoon in the Bois de Boulogne. The poor, on the other hand, were often simply evicted from their homes with no right to rehousing. And the new tenements that rose up beside Haussmann's wide, tree-lined boulevards may have looked like an improvement from the outside, but all too often their exteriors hid miserable overcrowding and

"People who have seen everything say that our sewers are perhaps the most beautiful things in the world. Light shines brilliantly, the slime keeps the temperature moderate, you can go boating, hunt rats..." CONTEMPORARY SATIRIST

BELOW **A 19th-century photograph of Charles Garnier's Opera House (1861–74), described when it was opened as having "pretty, ornamental detail, but no lines, no style, no grandeur." It was flagship buildings such as the Opera that appealed to Napoleon. Meanwhile, old overcrowded slums for the workers were replaced by new overcrowded slums.**

hard to repeat with the asphalt that replaced them. Along with the schools and churches, nine barracks were erected at key points around the city. In the east, the Canal Saint-Martin had long been a traditional defensive position for insurrectionists; deciding that a swing bridge over it would interfere with the line of one of his new boulevards, Haussmann covered over a mile-long section with another boulevard, mentioning that this would also allow Napoleon's troops to "take from behind all the faubourg Saint-Antoine."

Viewed individually, instances such as these amount to little. Together, they add up to architecture as class war: a sophisticated attempt to use town planning to subdue dissident elements of the population while retaining the support of the bourgeoisie, who were as scared as Napoleon of a return to the troubles of the 1830s and 1840s.

Like so many rulers, the Emperor's ambitions for Paris were nurtured by thoughts of Imperial Rome. "I want to be a second Augustus," he wrote in 1842, "for Augustus... made Rome a city of marble." There is a story that he once asked Edwin Chadwick what he thought of the rebuilt Paris. "Sir," replied the social reformer, "it was said of Augustus that he found Rome brick and left it marble. May it be said of you that you found Paris stinking and left it sweet." Not, perhaps, the memorial that Napoleon III hoped for. But at least he made the drains run on time.

BENITO MUSSOLINI AND THE EUR, ROME

Take the Via Cristoforo Columbo out of Rome towards Ostia, and you will soon find yourself driving through a grandiose if slightly dilapidated suburb. On every side there are wide avenues and monumental buildings, most of them obviously dating from the late 1930s. Some contain government offices and ministries; others house dusty museums, where guides try to interest groups of giggling schoolchildren in prehistoric pottery, agricultural implements, or fragments of Byzantine sculpture.

ABOVE **Benito Mussolini (1883–1945), whose vision of a third Rome to rival the glories of Italy's imperial and papal past led to the EUR. Would you buy a new world order from a man wearing this hat?**

OPPOSITE **The Palazzo della Civiltà Italiana (1938–43), the "square Colosseum" designed by the Rationalist architects Guerrini, La Padula, and Romano.**

Attendants at the Museo dell'Alto Medioevo or at the Museo Preistorico ed Etnografico will tell you that you have arrived at the Esposizione Universale di Roma (EUR), the site of what was almost the biggest world fair in history. They may or may not say that the EUR was intended as much more than just a world fair; in the words of its chief architect, Marcello Piacentini, it was to be "the great manifestation of Civilization that Italy will offer in the twentieth year of the Fascist Era... the monumental new quarter of Rome, the Capital of the Empire."

E42-XX, as the project was known – E for Esposizione, 42 for the year the fair was to take place, XX for the 20th anniversary of Benito Mussolini's seizure of power in 1922 – began life in June 1935 when Federico Pinna Berchet, who had worked on fairs at Milan and Padua, and Giuseppe Bottai, Mussolini's Governor of Rome, presented Il Duce with a proposal for a great exhibition, to be held on a site between Rome and Ostia. The idea fitted perfectly with Mussolini's long-cherished conception of a Fascist "third Rome" which stretched to the coast, building on the city's imperial and Christian past until, he said, it "spread over other hills, along the banks of the sacred river, reaching to the beaches of the

Tyrrhenian Sea." E42-XX, the most ambitious of all his building projects, would be an important stage in this process; from the first, the idea was to erect permanent buildings that would not only form the nucleus of a global "Olympics of Civilization," but also become a vital element in a *Roma nuovisssima*, the embodiment of Italy "with all the traditions of its past, the certainties of its present, and the anticipations of its future."

Expressing past, present, and future architecturally was a tall order. Increasingly during the 1930s, Mussolini drew parallels between the Fascist state and Imperial Rome, conjuring up the attractive notion (attractive to Italians, at least) that history might repeat itself and that aggressive Italian expansionism would result in a new Roman Empire. The obvious architectural style for this new empire was that of the old; and indeed, designs which reinterpreted classical themes appeared throughout the 1920s and early 1930s. But ironically, considering the fact that he could claim a more direct link with ancient Rome than most, Mussolini was more ambivalent towards classicism than either Hitler or Stalin. "We are the agents of a new type of civilization," he said. (And how right he was, although not in quite the way he intended.) And Rationalism, as the Modern Movement was called in pre-war Italy, also scored some notable successes, such as the uncompromising – and beautiful – Santa Maria Novella railway station in Florence, designed by Giovanni Michelucci and completed in 1933. Both Rationalists and Monumentalists claimed to be reinterpreting classicism; both assiduously courted Mussolini in the hope that their particular brand of architecture would be adopted by the Fascist regime to the exclusion of the other. But for much of the 1930s Il Duce happily endorsed both, unable to decide whether the associations with Italian Fascism's imperial ancestry was more important than the image of a modern industrial state that was being advanced by the Rationalists.

The earliest designs for the permanent buildings that make up the EUR reflect this indecision. As Superintendent of Architecture for the project, Piacentini sought a compromise of sorts; in the competition briefs that he wrote for the various buildings, he declared that the "classical and monumental spirit... which has been manifested and has endured through the centuries... must be the foundation, yet with the most modern and functional forms, of the architectural inspiration." So the grand entrance to the site on the Rome side was the Porta Imperiale of Giovanni Muzio, Mario Paniconi, and Giulio Pediconi, two three-storey crescents of columns and pillars that hark back unashamedly to Italy's imperial heritage; while on the Ostia side, Adalberto Libera designed a streamlined curving concrete Monumental Arch, a thoroughly Corbusian composition which would not have looked out of place in a sci-fi comic strip. Viewed along the main axis through the EUR, Libera's arch would have at the same time beckoned visitors into the complex and heralded Rome's march to Ostia and the sea.

"Would have," because by the late 1930s such an essay in pure Modernism proved too much for Italian Fascism, and the Monumental Arch was never built. Mussolini paid his first visit to

"It will be the great manifestation of Civilization that Italy will offer in the twentieth year of the Fascist era... the monumental new quarter of Rome, the Capital of the Empire." MARCELLO PIACENTINI, CHIEF ARCHITECT OF THE EUR

Germany in September 1937, and returned enormously impressed with everything Hitler showed him, including his own peculiar brand of monumental classicism. As his links with Hitler grew – their "Pact of Steel" was signed in May 1939, and Italy entered the war on Germany's side in June 1940 – Mussolini's desire to emulate and exceed the Nazis' cultural "achievements" grew too. His Manifesto of Racial Scientists, published in the summer of 1938, inaugurated a campaign of state-sanctioned anti-Semitism and, taking their cue from Hitler, his followers were quick to dismiss modernist art and architecture as the work of Jews, Bolsheviks, or worst of all, Bolshevik Jews. Although the debate continued into the early 1940s, the Rationalists who submitted competition entries for the various buildings of E42-XX were forced by the prevailing political climate to discard their initial dreams of a new Rome of concrete and glass and at least provide some clear cultural references to Italy's imperial glories. So, for

example, Libera's 1938 design for the Palazzo dei Congressi, a futuristic aeroplane hangar of a building, made concessions to the reactionary mood of the times by including a heavily stylized colonnade of stone pillars without capitals. The main square, the Piazza Imperiale (now the Piazza Marconi) was a collaborative effort by the Rationalists Luigi Moretti, Francesco Fariello, Saverio Muratori, and Ludovico Quaroni; yet it, too, draws on classical precedent through the use of stone colonnades and references to the Forums in Rome.

The most important building on the site was the Palazzo della Civiltà Italiana (1938–43), which was intended as the setting for a permanent exhibition of Italian culture from Augustus to Mussolini. The winning design came from another team of Rationalists – the architects Guerrini, La Padula, and Romano – who produced a six-storey structure over 60 metres (200 feet) high and nearly 60 metres (200 feet) square. Each of its four sides is devoid of decoration except for rows of huge open arches – 216 in all – in an obvious reference to one of the most famous of all classical buildings, the Colosseum in Rome. It was immediately christened "the square Colosseum," a nickname it retains to this day (see p.149).

The Palazzo quickly became the focus for the debate on what constituted an appropriate architecture in Mussolini's Fascist Italy. For some, the building was no more than "an architectural phantasm, an evocation, a stage set of stone and cement, not architecture." Its historicism and lack of integrity (the arches are purely cosmetic, a decorative skin placed over a concrete skeleton) fell uncomfortably between past and present, and even traditionally minded architects were profoundly uneasy about it. "To what reality can it testify?" asked Gio Ponti, a founder of the neoclassicist Novecento Movement. "When in future centuries historians address today's

BELOW **The Palazzo dei Congressi, designed by Adalberto Libera in 1938, is an uneasy compromise of aggressive Modernism tempered by classicism. By the end of the 1930s, Rationalist architects were forced to modify their ideas in order to conform to Mussolini's growing attachment to Hitlerian monumentalism.**

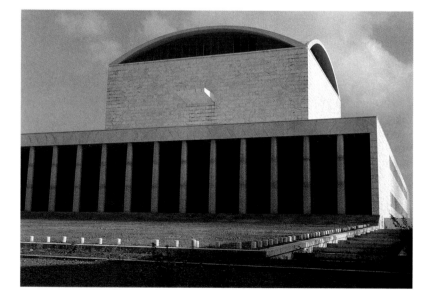

architecture... the Palazzo della Civiltà will leave them perplexed and disturbed." Others disagreed. "This fundamental element of our culture of builders [i.e. the arch]... is repeated perpetually like the fundamental elements of our millennial civilization itself." The Palazzo della Civiltà was pre-eminently a symbol of modern Italy, an Italy that remembered its majestic imperial past while simultaneously building an even more majestic future under Fascism.

Work on the Esposizione Universale di Roma ground to a halt in the wake of Mussolini's disastrous military campaigns of the early 1940s. The "Olympics of Civilization" that were to have opened on 21 April 1942, the supposed anniversary of the founding of Rome 27 centuries earlier, did not happen. It hardly seemed appropriate to celebrate 20 years of Fascist government in the wake of military defeats in Greece, in the Aegean, in North Africa, in the Mediterranean. Anyway, who would have come to the party? Many of the EUR's buildings were not completed until the 1950s, by which time Italy was anxious to distance itself from the relics of its Fascist past. But completed they were. Piacentini, one of Mussolini's favourite architects, was even rehabilitated to the extent that he collaborated in the design of the last major project for the site, the domed concrete Palazzo dello Sport which was built for the 1960 Rome Olympics.

The buildings of the EUR might easily be dismissed as crude historicism, every bit as distasteful as Hitler's megalomaniac fantasies for Berlin. They are distasteful, in that the taint of Fascism still lingers; the link between ideology and architecture can never be broken and should never be forgotten. But the EUR is neither crude, nor crudely historicist. It represents a rare and ultimately rather interesting attempt to unite Modernism and traditional architectural forms. And it is certainly a monument, a monument to Mussolini's horrifying vision of power. The groups of schoolchildren who traipse through its museums in the late 20th century would do well to remember that – if only because they are responsible for ensuring that it does not happen again.

ADOLF HITLER
AND **BERLIN**

One afternoon in 1938 Albert Speer, Hitler's personal architect, took his father to his offices in the old Berlin Academy of Arts on Pariser Platz. In closely guarded exhibition rooms which could only be entered with special permission from the Führer, he proudly showed the old man a huge model city, filled with residential and commercial buildings, factories, a new university, hospitals, and schools. Tiny trees and cars filled the streets, and fountains stood in the flower-lined squares.

ABOVE **Adolf Hitler (1889–1945) studies the plans for Berlin with his architect Albert Speer. He said, "The new city can be compared only to Babylon or Rome."**

OPPOSITE **The New Chancellery on Voss Strasse, designed by Speer in 1937. The materials used in the rapidly constructed building were produced in two concentration camps in Germany.**

At the heart of the model, more perfectly realized than the rest, lay a wide, straight boulevard. Around 30 metres (100 feet) long, it cut the city in two from north to south, stretching from a gigantic neoclassical railway station, under a monumental triumphal arch and on to a colossal domed hall at its northern end.

This was Adolf Hitler's vision of Berlin: a new metropolis that would stand for a thousand years; a city which men would mention in the same breath as Babylon and Rome. Speer's father gazed at the model for some moments. "You've all gone completely crazy," he said, and walked out.

When Hitler became Chancellor in 1933, his plans to transform Berlin into a great modern capital seemed to be grounded in common sense. Most Berliners agreed when he announced that the city was "an unsystematic collection or unsystematic series of residential and commercial buildings"; most Germans applauded his intention to raise their capital "to such a high level of urban planning and culture that it may compete with all the other capital cities of the world." After all, Berlin's basic street pattern had been laid out back in 1862, when it was still only a provincial centre; although it had become the headquarters of the newly unified Germany nine years later, its

infrastructure had failed to keep pace with a rate of growth that surpassed that of any other European capital, with a population which had risen from 826,000 in 1871 to well over four million in 1925. Attempts at modernization during the 1910s and 1920s had come to nothing, although Hitler's own vision probably had its roots in one of them; at a 1927 art exposition in the city Martin Mächler had exhibited a scheme for reorganizing the city along its north-south axis, and lining the new boulevard thus created with government buildings. Hitler's plans bear a striking resemblance to Mächler's.

Hitler was initially content to leave the modernization of Berlin to the municipal authorities. However, the City Council was anxious about both the finance for the project and the practicalities involved in resiting factories and rehousing hundreds of thousands of people, and as a result the mayor, Julius Lippert, was constantly trying to tone down Hitler's proposals. By the summer of 1936 the Führer's patience was exhausted, and he decided to hand the project over to Albert Speer, then a rising star in the Party, who had already designed a number of district headquarters for the Nazis and had remodelled the official Berlin residences of Goebbels and Göring. Speer's

commissions had also included the stage sets for two big Party rallies: one at Berlin's Templehof Field, where he produced a backdrop to the main platform consisting of three banners, each higher than a ten-storey building, illuminated by powerful searchlights; and a second at Zeppelin Field in Nuremberg (see p.154) for the Party's first rally in government, with a centrepiece consisting of an eagle with a wingspan of 30 metres (100 feet).

Speer's ability to produce triumphalist drama appealed to the Führer. In 1937 he was also given the job of designing a new Chancellery on Voss Strasse (see right), and came up with a scheme for a succession of state rooms that forced visiting diplomats to walk nearly 250 metres (750 feet), traversing a gallery twice the length of the Hall of Mirrors at Versailles, before they finally arrived at Hitler's reception hall. "On the long walk from the entrance... they'll get a taste of the power and grandeur of the German Reich," a delighted Hitler exclaimed when he saw the plans.

Speer assembled a huge team of architects and planners, painters and sculptors to work on the Berlin project. There was to be a new railway system, airports, a university quarter, a medical quarter with hospitals, medical schools, and laboratories. But in Hitler's mind, the focus of the whole scheme was always the Grand Avenue that ran 5 kilometres (3 miles) from a main railway station bigger than New York's Grand Central to a triumphal arch 168 metres (550 feet) wide and twice the height of the Arc de Triomphe. From there it moved on past theatres and cinemas, restaurants and hotels, until it reached the new government quarter and its 11 ministries, three secretariats, the Chancellery, the High Command of the Armed Forces, the Reichstag – and a Chancellor's residence that alone occupied 2 million square metres (22 million square feet).

But even Hitler's palace was dwarfed by the Great Hall that was to tower over Adolf Hitler Platz at the northern termination of the avenue.

ABOVE **A wall of searchlights forms a backdrop to a Nazi Party rally at Zeppelin Field at Nuremburg in September 1937. Albert Speer's ability to produce suitable settings for Hitler's triumphalist rhetoric led to his appointment as architect for the reconstruction of Berlin.**

Conceived by the Führer himself as a venue for indoor rallies, it was designed to hold more than 150,000 people under a copper dome that rose 221 metres (726 feet) into the sky. The central skylight would be 46 metres (152 feet) in diameter – more than wide enough for the whole dome of St Peter's in Rome to pass through it (see opposite). For the Führer's 48th birthday Speer presented him with a scale model of the Hall; for his 50th in April 1939, another of the triumphal arch. They were kept along with all the other models in Speer's offices at the Academy of Arts, and gradually the galleries in Pariser Platz came to resemble a vast toytown, with spotlights on important buildings and a system of lighting which could simulate the effect of the sun at different times of the day. A special entrance was cut through from the Chancellery gardens, and late at night Hitler and his entourage would come to admire the scheme and enquire after its progress. The Führer spent hours peering down his avenue from the railway station, looking at it from different angles, imagining the effect it would have on visiting dignitaries. When one finally enters the Reich Chancellery, he told Bormann and Himmler, "...one should have the feeling that one is visiting the master of the world."

Hitler's conception of public architecture, like Speer's articulation of it, was both simple and simplistic; size was what mattered. The biggest was by definition the best, and he was devastated to discover that Stalin's Palace of the Soviets in Moscow was to be even bigger than his Great Hall. (After he invaded Russia in June 1941 he told Speer that "this will be the end of their building for good and all.") As his megalomania grew, he increasingly came to identify the buildings on the Grand Avenue with his own personal power. He constantly pushed Speer to keep to schedule and complete the project by 1950; sooner or later he would die, and the task he had set himself, to create a Reich to last for a thousand years, would fall to successors who would inevitably be weaker, less charismatic figures. Such men would need the prestige given by association with the first Reichsführer. "That is why we must complete this construction in my lifetime – so that I shall have lived [in the new palace] and my spirit will have conferred tradition upon the building. If I live in it only for a few years, that will be good enough."

Speer did his best to comply. In the spring of 1939, work began on clearing away old buildings and landscaping vast areas. Displaced Berliners – the racially pure Aryans, at least – were rehoused by Speer's "Main Resettlement Division," a partnership with the Gestapo that sought to register the 82,000 Jews living in the capital, evict them, and give their apartments to those who had been made homeless by the reconstruction work. But although a number of minor buildings were actually completed, the outbreak of war in September effectively brought the scheme to a halt. A projected total cost of between four and six billion Reichsmarks was difficult enough to justify even

"Why always the biggest? I do this to restore to each individual German his self-respect. In a hundred areas I want to say to the individual: We are not inferior; on the contrary, we are the complete equals of every other nation." ADOLF HITLER AT A RALLY FOR CONSTRUCTION WORKERS (1938)

in a peacetime dictatorship; in wartime it was completely untenable. Even so, Hitler retained his dream almost to the end, cherishing fantasies of the speeches he would one day give in the Great Hall at the heart of his capital, which after the war was to be renamed "Germania."

In his memoirs, Speer recalled how in dismissing the petty objections of his Finance Minister, Hitler had predicted that the income from tourism would pay many times over for the Great Hall, the new palace, and all the other state buildings on the Grand Avenue. "Remember what happened with Ludwig II. Everyone said he was mad because of the cost of his palaces. But today?... The entrance fees alone have long since paid for the building costs." What Hitler did not appreciate is that Ludwig of Bavaria *was* mad.

BELOW **Speer's model of the Great Hall that was to dominate Adolf Hitler Platz at the northern end of Berlin's Grand Avenue. It was designed to hold 150,000 of the Party faithful – the cupola that capped the dome would have been wider than the dome of St Peter's in Rome.**

ABOVE **The neoclassicist Red Army Theatre by Alabian and Simbirtsev (1935). It was inconveniently designed in the shape of a star, an example of how symbolism became more important than function in the state architecture of this period.**

Vladimir Tatlin's astonishing design for a Monument to the Third International had set the tone in 1919; a helter-skelter spiral of iron mesh which enclosed three constantly revolving glass chambers – a cube, a pyramid, and a cylinder – it epitomized the avant-garde's determination to turn its back on history. Although it went no further than the model stage, the Tatlin Tower remained an inspiration to a generation of Soviet architects who deliberately rejected precedent in their desire to forge a brave new world and who, if they were not prepared to go quite as far as Tatlin, were still at the leading edge of world architecture. A few examples can serve for many: the Vesnin brothers' pioneering Constructivist

The government advised "Research should be directed at using both new and also the best elements of classical architecture." The Party newspaper, *Izvestiya*, went further; the palace must "incorporate the whole cultural inheritance of the past."

design for a Palace of Labour (1923) which, like the Tatlin Tower, remained unbuilt; Konstantin Melnikov's reinforced concrete and glass Rusakov Club for Transport Workers (1928); the uncompromisingly Modernist *Pravda* building designed by Pantelemon Golosov in 1929; and the equally uncompromising Moscow Planetarium of Mikhail Barshch and Mikhail Siniavskii (1929), a steel-framed dome rising above a rigidly geometrical concrete lower floor.

In the excitement following the Revolution, it seemed that anything was possible, and the dynamic creative potential offered by Soviet society in the 1920s even drew leading foreign talent to Moscow; Hannes Meyer, Walter Gropius's replacement as director of the Bauhaus, left Germany to work in the city in 1930, while Le Corbusier, whose severe rationalism influenced many of the new Soviet architects, was a regular visitor as a result of his competition-winning design with a sheer glass facade for the new offices of the Central Union of Consumer Societies offices in 1928.

But the dream died – in more ways than one, of course. The tight hold on every aspect of Soviet society which figured so large in Stalin's thinking during the 1930s was incompatible with artistic freedom, and with the formation in 1932 of the state-controlled Organization of the Union of Soviet Architects, the years of experiment were over. With supreme irony Stalin, the man at the helm of the most radical revolution the world had ever known, was deeply conservative at heart; and it was his personal tastes – at first for a rather vague monumental classicism of the sort favoured by Hitler, and later for a decidedly kitsch Russian baroque – that were to dominate the Moscow skyline in the 1930s and 1940s.

The first step in the imposition of Stalinist culture was taken in 1931, with the announcement of a competition for the Palace of the Soviets, a new seat of government and the single most important building in the entire Soviet Union. The site that was chosen, on the north bank of the River Moskva, was occupied by the 19th-century Cathedral of Christ the Saviour. As one of Stalin's leading architects, Boris Iofan, was quick to point out, the cathedral "symbolizes the power and the taste of the lords of old Moscow." It was blown up on 5 December 1931 to make way for the new palace.

Hundreds of designs, including schemes by Gropius and Le Corbusier, were submitted for Stalin's consideration. But anything too aggressively modern was discarded. In drawing up a short list for further development, the government advised entrants that "research should be directed at using both new and also the best elements of classical architecture." The Party newspaper, *Izvestiya*, went further, stating that the palace must "incorporate the whole cultural inheritance of the past."

In the end, the competition was won by Iofan. In close collaboration with Stalin himself, he evolved a scheme which – had it ever been completed – would have been the largest building in the world. The site occupied 110,000 square metres (1,184,000 square feet), while the Palace itself was to be more than 300 metres (984 feet) high, and plastered with pillars, inspirational statues, and classical carvings. Inside there were two halls capable of seating 20,000 and 8,000 people, restaurants, offices, and other amenities intended to accommodate meetings of the Supreme Soviet, Party congresses and the like. And on Stalin's personal orders an initial plan for the structure to be

BELOW **The Moskva Hotel on Gorky Street, designed by Aleksei Shchusev in 1935. The asymmetrical wings are said to have been built because Stalin was presented with two variant designs. Not understanding the plans, he approved them both – and no-one dared to contradict him.**

CHAPTER 7

PRESTIGE IN A DEMOCRATIC AGE

THE AT&T BUILDING, NEW YORK

The skyscraper is the 20th century's greatest contribution to the architecture of power, a perfect marriage of capitalist hubris and construction technology. Since 1885, when William Le Baron Jenney pioneered the use of a load-carrying structural frame in his nine-storey Home Insurance Building in Chicago, the skeletal steel frame, coupled with the development of safe passenger-lifts at the end of the century, has resulted in towering corporate headquarters and office complexes in every major city on earth.

ABOVE **Philip Johnson, the architect of the AT&T building. Although he started out as an ardent propagandist for the Modern Movement, by the 1970s Johnson had come to reject the rigid aesthetics of Modernism.**

OPPOSITE **The AT&T is a mix of references. The entrance arch, flanked by rectangular openings, recalls Brunelleschi's Pazzi Chapel, while the vertical bands above it quote from a late 19th-century high-rise.**

By 1908, Ernest Flagg's 47-storey Beaux-Arts Singer Tower loomed over Broadway in New York. It was 204 metres (670 feet) high – nearly 80 metres (262 feet) taller than the Great Pyramid and 35 metres (115 feet) taller than the Washington Monument. Five years later the Singer was overtaken by Cass Gilbert's neogothic "cathedral of commerce," the 241.5 metre (792 foot) Woolworth Building, also on Broadway. For a few months between 1930 and 1931, the Art Deco Chrysler Building by William van Alen (319 metres/1047 feet) held the title of the tallest man-made structure on earth, only to be topped by the most famous skyscraper of them all, William Lamb's 381 metre (1250 foot) Empire State Building. By 1998 the tallest building in the world (453 metres/1486 feet) was Cesar Pelli's Petronas Towers in Kuala Lumpur, the headquarters of Malaysia's national petroleum corporation.

When the American Telephone and Telegraph Company (AT&T) decided in the autumn of 1975 to build a new high-rise headquarters at 550 Madison Avenue in New York, it was following a well-established tradition of corporate monumentalism. The board chairman, John deButts, did not want the tallest building in the world, but he wanted something unique – not quite such an obvious statement as it seems. The bronze Seagram Building on Park Avenue by Mies van der Rohe and Philip Johnson (1954–8; see p.9) had spawned a whole generation of plain metal-and-glass Modernist slabs which were often designed by architects with none of Mies's genius and none of Johnson's flair for the theatrical. DeButts respected the Seagram – who wouldn't? – and wanted the new AT&T Building to match it in architectural quality. Nevertheless, he did not want another glass box.

After approaching 25 of America's leading architects for their ideas, deButts and the AT&T board chose the partnership of Johnson/Burgee. Philip Johnson, much the more established of the two men, was now in his early 70s, with a distinguished career as a Modernist architect behind him. After a period in the 1930s as the director of the Architecture Department at the Museum of Modern Art (MoMA), where he was an ardent propagandist for the International Style of Le Corbusier and Mies, he had set up his own highly successful practice in the 1940s. Over the following years an enthusiasm for spectacle (and for publicity) led him to question the functionalist puritanism of Modernism – "Can't we just wander round aimlessly?" he asked rather

An absurdly kitsch statue was placed in the entrance lobby... a naked, golden, winged male, perches atop a globe, clutching three lightning bolts in one hand and a roll of electric cable in the other, like a camp household deity – Cellini's Perseus meets the Village People.

BELOW **Corporate magnificence in the Sky Lobby, an area restricted to AT&T personnel. Simple geometrical forms, all executed in marble, produce an effect of Byzantine opulence.**

plaintively in 1960. His more recent buildings, while still acknowledging their debt to the European functionalists, had exhibited a playfulness and a use of elements from the past that would doubtless have astonished the Johnson who had introduced the Modern Movement to America with his famous "Modern Architecture: International Exhibition" at MoMA in 1932.

The basis of the design by Johnson and Burgee was a 203-metre (666-foot) high rectangular block (see p.167). It was to be no sub-Miesian slab, however. In fact, deButts got all the uniqueness he wanted and more, in the form of a plethora of non-functional cultural references

that infuriated the purists and delighted press and public. The architects adopted a tripartite arrangement of clearly defined base, shaft, and decorated capital, which had been common during the early history of the skyscraper; and in place of the then-prevalent curtain wall of glass, they opted for a cladding of rose-grey granite from the same quarry that supplied the facing for Grand Central Station. Most of the base is taken up with an open loggia; the whole structure is raised 20 metres (67 feet) above street-level on huge piers, leaving a public plaza below, which Johnson said reminded him of an Egyptian hypostyle hall (a hall with a roof supported by many columns). Above, the recessed tiers of windows behind vertical bands recall Louis Sullivan's Guaranty Building in Buffalo, New York (1894–5), one of the first great skyscrapers.

The entrance consists of a round-headed arch 35 metres (115 feet) high, flanked on either side by three 20-metre (66-foot) high rectangular openings. The composition pays homage to Renaissance classicism; Johnson said that it derived from the facade of Filippo Brunelleschi's Pazzi Chapel at Santa Croce in Florence (1429), while critics have seen in it references to the Palladian window and, less kindly, to the pre-war Fascist reinterpretation of classicism of the Italian Rationalists. The central arch leads into a vaulted, vaguely Romanesque lobby with a black-and-white marble floor taken from the early 20th-century British architect Edwin Lutyens, and, until it was removed a few years ago, an absurdly kitsch statue, the *Spirit of Communication* (see p.1). A naked, golden, winged male perches atop a globe, clutching three lightning bolts in one hand and a roll of electric cable in the other, like a camp household deity – Cellini's Perseus meets the Village People. The figure, by Evelyn Longman, had crowned an earlier AT&T Building; Johnson persuaded deButts to rescue it and install it in the lobby.

Elevators take the visitor up to the marble main lobby on the first floor; their decoration, inspired by the Art Deco lifts in the Chrysler Building, completes the bewildering mélange of historical quotations – with one important exception. The Woolworth had its spires and pinnacles, the Chrysler its gleaming metallic sunbursts. And in a move that ensured that the AT&T would be one of the most talked-about buildings of the decade, Johnson decided on a return to the early 20th-century practice of capping New York skyscrapers with elaborate crowns. So the AT&T was given a colossal broken pediment which was meant, perhaps, to conjure up the baroque or to reinvent the classical cornices of late 19th-century office blocks; but which in fact invited comparison with a Rolls-Royce radiator, a longcase clock, and a Chippendale highboy (see right).

Reactions to the AT&T Building were mixed, but everybody reacted. "Postmodernism's major monument," claimed one critic. "A pastiche of historical references," said another. The design appeared on the front page of the *New York Times*, *Time* magazine, and even the London *Times*. Every element was deconstructed, decoded – and sometimes derided – as do-it-yourself history, undiluted Postmodernist irony, a profound reading of the skyscraper's corporate and civic obligations.

"[It] may have its humorous aspects," said Johnson, "but you'll know it's our building." More importantly for deButts and the AT&T, people would know it was *their* building. In the forest of glass boxes that passed for commercial architecture in midtown Manhattan, the AT&T stood out, providing the company with a symbolic if slightly perplexing identity. And if the message it sent out to corporate America was not altogether clear – "We subscribe to traditional values"? "We build a new future on the lessons of the past"? "We make furniture"? – that message was at least writ large. There is only one thing worse than being talked about, and that is not being talked about.

Sadly, the building's career as AT&T's corporate headquarters proved short-lived. In 1974 the United States government had begun an anti-trust suit against AT&T's domination of the US telecommunications network; and on 1 January 1984, less than a year after the Chippendale skyscraper was completed, AT&T divested itself of its Bell operating companies, which provided local exchange services. At a stroke, the corporation lost two-thirds of its one million employees, and 77 per cent of its $149 million assets. Such radical down-sizing meant that the AT&T Building was no longer appropriate; in 1992 the company moved out and, sadly, the *Spirit of Communication* went with them. The Sony Corporation took the Madison Avenue tower on a 20-year lease and renamed it the Sony Building. But as far as history is concerned it remains the AT&T Building, a powerful testament to Johnson/Burgee's vision of a new, more entertaining corporate America.

ABOVE **The broken pediment at the top of the AT&T building that caused all the fuss and earned it the nickname of "the Chippendale skyscraper." "It may have its humorous aspects," said Johnson, "but you'll know it's our building."**

FRANÇOIS MITTERRAND AND PARIS

"Yes, I like history, and I like leaving traces of history," said François Mitterrand in 1995. "People remember Tutankhamun. What will they say in a few thousand years of Charles de Gaulle, Georges Pompidou, Valérie Giscard d'Estaing – of me?" There is no doubt that a big ego and a desire to leave "traces of history" were important motives behind the *grands projets de l'état*, the major architectural programme for Paris that Mitterrand initiated and personally supervised during the 1980s.

ABOVE **François Mitterrand (1916–96). His 14-year stint as President of France made him the longest-serving head of state since Napoleon III, and his contribution to the architectural character of Paris was infinitely more exciting than the Emperor's.**

But there were worthier motives. As a socialist (albeit a rather luke-warm one), Mitterrand was convinced of the propriety of state patronage of architecture. He was eager to provide a series of setpieces for the Bicentennial celebrations of the French Revolution in 1989. And, most important of all, he wanted to imbue the French with a sense of their own culture, "so that the nation can identify itself once more."

The most famous of the *grands projets* is the extension to the Louvre. When Mitterrand came to power in 1981 the old royal palace, which had been an art museum since the Revolution, was no longer serving its purpose. Public collections were housed on different levels in one wing beside the Seine, with the Ministry of Finance occupying the Richelieu wing to the north. There was inadequate storage space, and visitors were so bewildered by the labyrinth of staircases and galleries that three out of four could not even find the collections on the upper floors.

I. M. Pei, the Chinese-American architect commissioned to solve the problem, proposed to eject the Ministry of Finance and extend the museum into the Richelieu wing, while leaving its neo-Renaissance Second Empire facade intact. A new complex of visitor services was to be housed

in a 200 by 120 metre (656 by 394 foot) space underneath the court formed by the two wings, the Cour Napoléon. This left the historic exterior of the Louvre virtually untouched – with one significant exception. Pei's treatment of the entrance to the underground complex involved building a clear glass pyramid, 22 metres (72 feet) high and 35 metres (114 feet) square, smack in the centre of the Cour Napoléon.

In 1984 Pei's scheme was presented to the Commission Supérieure des Monuments Historiques, which vetted projects that might impinge on national monuments. Although the plans were passed, several Commissioners were appalled by the pyramid, whipping up a storm of protest in the media. Conservationists condemned the design for not being in keeping with its surroundings; modernists condemned it for not being sufficiently modern; and xenophobes condemned it for not being French. One senior civil servant was quoted by *Le Figaro* as saying how "surprised" he was "that they have brought in a Chinese architect from America to handle the development of the historic core of the capital of France"; and after another newspaper carried an attack on Mitterrand and the pyramid with the headline, "Who does he think he is, Rameses II?,"

the rest of the press dubbed the President "Mitterramsès." Nevertheless, his personal backing for the scheme ensured its completion. "I could not have done anything without him," Pei later recalled.

Mitterrand's faith and Pei's genius have been amply vindicated. The pyramid startles without offending; its relatively small scale and its clean simplicity provide a strong central focus for the outlying galleries without overwhelming them (see p.173); and the cultural reference to Napoleon's conquest of Egypt is somehow playful rather than bombastic. It is a mark of its success that even the ultra-conservative (in architectural matters, at least) Prince of Wales has given the

ABOVE **The Islamic-influenced pierced metal screens of the Institut du Monde Arabe (Jean Nouvel, 1987–8), a Franco-Arab cultural centre and one of Mitterrand's *grands projets*.**

LEFT **The chromium-nickel Géode at La Villette. The Omnimax cinema, which seems to float in a pool of water, is part of the biggest science and technology centre in the world.**

ABOVE **The Grande Arche at La Défense (1983–9, by Johann Otto von Spreckelsen), which terminates the main western axis through Paris made by the Louvre, the Champs Elysées and avenue Charles de Gaulle. It was described by its architect as "humanity's triumphal arch."**

part to the 19th-century monumentalism of Jean-François Chalgrin's Arc de Triomphe 3 kilometres (1.9 miles) away. Faced in Carrara marble, it seems from a distance to be a massive rectangular arch with deeply chamfered edges, leading the viewer into La Défense and suggesting by its openness a continuation of the city's main axis westward. But the Grande Arche is functional as well as monumental. The two sides contain narrow office blocks 35 storeys high; and the horizontal member consists of exhibition spaces surrounding four open rooftop courtyards. Von Spreckelsen described the building as "humanity's triumphal arch"; perhaps it would be more accurate to call it a homage to late 20th-century commerce, just as its counterpart on the place Charles de Gaulle is a celebration of the First Empire's military might.

Many of the public buildings put up during Mitterrand's presidency have already become Parisian icons. Besides the Louvre pyramid and the Grande Arche, there is the much-photographed Géode in the north-east of Paris – an Omnimax cinema housed in a chromium-nickel steel sphere 36 metres (118 feet) in diameter (see p.171). It was built on the site of partly completed slaughterhouses that De Gaulle had rather tastelessly announced as "an abattoir for the year 2000."

Admittedly, not all the *grands projets* were equally successful. The Institut du Monde Arabe (p.171), which houses a Franco-Arab cultural centre, is relatively unobtrusive, even dull, relying for its effect on a huge array of rectangular windows with metal grills that recall the geometrical openwork of Islamic screens. And Dominique Perrault's Bibliothèque Nationale (1989–96) is striking, certainly; yet the open-book symbolism of the four L-plan glass towers facing each other across a sunken central court seems somewhat literal-minded. The Opéra de la Bastille, a new opera house for the people which was one of the first projects announced by Mitterrand after a

pyramid his cautious approval, describing its proportions as "pleasing" and saying that the French had shown "great taste."

"I am attracted by pure, geometrical shapes," Mitterrand once said; and like Pei's glass pyramid, the Grande Arche which terminates the vista through La Défense reflects his preferences. Conceived in the 1950s as a new commercial and residential centre, La Defénse was not a particularly prepossessing development, suffering from a surfeit of mediocre 1960s high-rise office blocks. In 1983 an international competition was held for a symbolic termination to the western axis through the city; the winning design (see above), by the Danish architect Johann Otto von Spreckelsen, offered an uncompromisingly modern counter-

1981 governmental review of music in the capital, has also received its fair share of criticism, not least because its rectangular black entrance and pale green glass-and-ceramic facade were felt to lack impact (for which, read pomp and grandeur). However, the design, an international competition-winner (as was the Bibliothèque Nationale) by the Canadian architect Carlos Ott – and personally selected by Mitterrand (again, like the Bibliothèque) – was kept deliberately simple, emphasizing the President's desire that this opera house, in contrast to Napoleon III's grandiose Opéra Garnier (see p.147), was for ordinary people. It was opened by Mitterrand on 13 July 1989, the eve of the 200th anniversary of the storming of the Bastille.

Not since the Second Empire has Paris seen the appearance of so many interesting public buildings; not since the reign of Louis XIV has France seen civic architecture of such high quality. With the *grands projets* Mitterrand managed to create a climate in which good modern architecture could thrive within the historic city without destroying it, in which debate moved things forward rather than backward, in which a sense of national cultural identity could be fostered without falling back on historicist pastiche. Other European capitals should take note.

Mitterrand's personal backing for the Louvre scheme ensured its completion. "I could not have done anything without him," Pei later recalled.

ABOVE **I. M. Pei's glass pyramid in the Cour Napoléon at the Louvre, the crowning glory of Mitterrand's *grands projets d'état*. Even the Prince of Wales liked it.**

THE SULTAN OF BRUNEI AND THE ISTANA NURUL IMAN

"Government Continues to Provide Bruneians with Comfortable Accommodation." The headline, in a November 1997 edition of the *Brunei Daily News*, leads into a story about how housing schemes by the government of His Majesty the Sultan and Yang Di-Pertuan of Brunei Darussalam have built more than 4000 three- and four-bedroomed houses in recent years, at heavily subsidized prices ranging from $52,000 to $95,000 – an impressive achievement for a country of only 300,000 people.

ABOVE **The Sultan and Yang Di-Pertuan of Brunei Darussalam (b.1946). Brunei, one of the richest countries in the world, is smaller than one of the Sultan's Australian cattle ranches.**

OPPOSITE **The golden archway leading to the Throne Room at the Istana Nurul Iman, the Palace of the Light of Faith. The room can hold 2000 people, and the light is provided by the 12 biggest chandeliers in the world.**

But it pales beside the comfortable accommodation which Hassanal Bolkiah, the 29th Sultan of Brunei, built for himself in the early 1980s. His Istana Nurul Iman, or "Palace of the Light of Faith," which lies on a low hill overlooking the capital, Bandar Seri Begawan, is the largest private residence in the world.

The Sultanate of Negara Brunei Darussalam, to give Brunei its full name, is a tiny country on the north-west coast of Borneo, completely surrounded to the south by the Malaysian state of Sarawak. It occupies an area of 5770 square kilometres (2228 square miles), rather less than one of the Sultan's Australian cattle ranches. In 1929, oil was discovered at Seria Town, to the west of Bandar Seri Begawan. Three years later Shell began commercial production, which by 1956 had risen to 114,700 barrels a day. Around the same time, offshore surveys discovered significant new fields, and Brunei was on its way to becoming one of the richest nations on earth. Today, a net worth of around $38 billion and a daily income measured in tens of millions of dollars make Hassanal Bolkiah the only man in the world whose wealth rivals that of software tycoon Bill Gates.

The Sultan came to power in 1967 at the age of 21, after the abdication of his father. Omar Ali Saifuddien III was an able politician, who successfully negotiated a measure of internal independence from Britain in 1959. (The country had been a British protectorate since 1888.) He also prevented British attempts to relegate Brunei to the status of just another province of the newly formed Malaysian Federation, in a clever series of manoeuvres that led to the curious spectacle of the Foreign Office trying to persuade the protectorate to accept full independence, and the Sultan adamant that it must remain under British control. Full independence was finally granted (and accepted) in 1984, but without any of the political debate or civil unrest that accompanied similar transfers of power in the rest of the Empire. In the early 1960s Omar Ali Saifuddien had experimented briefly with democratic elections; the rebellion that followed in 1962 was put down by a battalion of Gurkhas, and ever since then Brunei has been an absolute monarchy, with sole power vested in the Sultan as head of state, prime minister, commander-in-chief of the armed forces, and arbiter on all religious matters. Hassanal Bolkiah's attitude mirrors that of his father. Soon after independence, a *Newsweek* interviewer asked whether he would now allow free political activity. He said, "We have tried it.

ABOVE **This courtyard, with its fountains that operate 24 hours a day, is a modern take on a traditional Islamic architectural feature.**

BELOW **The Istana Nurul Iman, with 1788 rooms covering an area of more than 1 square kilometre (0.4 square mile), is the largest residential building in the world. The domes are covered with 22-carat gold leaf.**

We had elections before 1962 and we had a few political parties, but people competed against each other and chaos resulted."

Not surprisingly, Brunei's post-war wealth has found an expression in architecture. There are the inevitable bland high-rises, local headquarters of banks and multi-national corporations, which have sprung up in Bandar Seri Begawan over the last couple of decades, as they have all over south-east Asia. But there are also other, more interesting buildings. Omar Ali Saifuddien's major architectural monument is the spectacular mosque which bears his name, and which was completed in 1958. Created by Italian architects, it follows a classic Islamic design, with raw materials and furnishings imported from all over the world – mosaics of Venetian glass for the golden dome, Italian marble and Shanghai granite, carpets from Belgium and Saudi Arabia, stained glass windows and chandeliers from the United Kingdom.

Hassanal Bolkiah has outdone his father as a patron of architecture. As well as the Jame' Asr Hassanal Bolkiah Mosque, built to commemorate the 25th anniversary of the Sultan's accession and the largest mosque in Brunei, he has commis-

sioned schools, a university, the Jerudong theme park, a commercial centre and shopping mall, housing, road networks, an international airport, hospitals, and clinics. But while in recent years the Brunei government's spin doctors have tended to play up the Sultan's religious and public works, his most awe-inspiring contribution to the architecture of power remains his own home, the Istana Nurul Iman.

The Istana Nurul Iman is one of those places which seems to exist as a collection of "amazing facts," a statistical rather than an architectural object. It cost B$1.3 billion to build, or around US$4 million. It contains 1788 rooms and occupies over 1 square kilometre (0.4 square mile). There are more than 3 kilometres (1.9 miles) of underground passages. The Throne Room, which can hold 2000 people (see p.175), is lit by 12 enormous chandeliers, each weighing 2000 kilogrammes (4410 pounds) and each costing $640,000. The 300-car indoor parking lot is air-conditioned, and so are the stables for the Sultan's polo ponies. The stories of fabulous luxury are legion: the gold fittings on the palace's two domes, in the throne room, in the bathrooms, even in the helicopter that the Sultan uses to travel around the country; the 2000 telephones; the 110 sports cars and custom-built, gold-plated stretch limos. The palace is closed to the public except at the end of Ramadan, when the royal family greet their subjects.

Opinions on Hassanal Bolkiah and the Istana Nurul Iman tend to fall into two camps. On the one hand, there are those who say that the Sultan is an autocratic absolutist whose time has passed, and whose colossal palace is the epitome of bad taste and new wealth. On the other, there are those who see him as an enlightened ruler who is gently easing his people into the 21st century, and who regard the Istana as a stabilizing influence, a visible presence that helps to confirm the patriarchal status quo, and to relieve the need to resort to repression and state-sanctioned violence. The truth is more complicated. Bruneians are certainly disenfranchised; their relationship to their head of state is deferential to the point of being feudal. Yet against all liberal Western preconceptions they are infuriatingly happy, with good, tax-free incomes, free education, and free health care. The crime rate is one of the lowest in the world. There is an average of two televisions and almost four cars per household. Even the rides at the Jerudong theme park are free to all.

So, in a supposedly democratic age, what does the Palace of the Light of Faith represent? How is one to interpret the prestigious Istana, with its sweeping roofs, its fountains and mosaics, the staggering opulence of everything from state rooms to bathrooms? Architecturally, it has to be said that the palace is not particularly distinguished. Ideologically, its arrogance is frankly indefensible. As an argument for late 20th-century materialism, an awesome reminder that in the right hands money can buy happiness – not just for an individual, but for a whole society – it challenges everything that Western democracies hold dear. And perhaps as a symbol, it warns us that everything has a price. Even liberty.

ABOVE **The gold-encrusted Council Chamber at the Palace. The Sultan is absolute ruler of Brunei. He once said, when asked about his thoughts on free elections, "We have tried it... we had a few political parties, but people competed against each other and chaos resulted."**

The stories of fabulous luxury are legion: the gold fittings on the palace's two domes, in the throne room, in the bathrooms, even in the helicopter that the Sultan uses to travel around the country; the 2000 telephones; the 110 sports cars and custom-built, gold-plated stretch limos.

PRINCE CHARLES AND POUNDBURY

The critics have not been kind to Poundbury, the Prince of Wales' model village on the outskirts of Dorchester. The cobbled streets, the blend of brick, stone, and stucco housing, the sash windows, stone mullions, and old-fashioned lamps have been dismissed as reactionary historicism, condemned as an example of pandering to popularism, censured as an inappropriately un-English piece of urbanism imposed on the Dorset landscape and laughed at as a mixture of Disneyland and Toytown.

ABOVE **The Prince of Wales (b.1948) has taken an active role in promoting the use of traditional architectural styles in contemporary building.**

OPPOSITE, ABOVE AND BELOW **Model housing at Poundbury, the village outside Dorchester in Dorset created by the Prince of Wales and Leon Krier. Comforting reactionary historicism, or a solution to the problem of suburban housing in the 1990s?**

But Charleyville, as the estate is known locally, also has its admirers. Traditionalist architects and conservative polemicists have leaped to its defence. So have members of the public, who prefer the comfortably small scale, the diverse yet familiar vernacular styles of the houses, and the sense of being in control of their environment that comes with a strong element of consultation and community involvement. The project has generated strong feelings on both sides, and by the time the first cottages, houses, and flats went on sale in 1994, the 162-hectare (400-acre) building site had become a battleground, as Modernists and traditionalists engaged in a passionate debate over the way ahead for British architecture.

The man whose brainchild Poundbury was has been one of the nation's most strident opponents of Modernism since the early 1980s. One of the Prince of Wales' first public pronouncements on the subject came in the autumn of 1984, at a dinner to celebrate the 150th anniversary of the Royal Institute of British Architects. He used the occasion to criticize the proposed extension to William Wilkins' Greek Revival National Gallery in London, calling it a "monstrous carbuncle on the face of a much-loved and elegant friend"; it was eventually scrapped in favour of a loosely classical scheme by the father of Postmodernism, Robert Venturi. The Prince followed up with other attacks on modernist architecture. A tower designed by Ludwig Mies van der Rohe and planned for a prestigious site next to the Mansion House in the City of London was "a glass stump" (see p.180). Proposals for the redevelopment of Paternoster Square, a rather nasty post-war precinct just to the north of St Paul's, did not give due weight to Wren's cathedral: "I would... like to see the kinds of materials Wren might have used – soft red brick and stone dressing perhaps, and the ornament and detail of classical architecture, but on a scale humble enough not to compete with the monumentality of St Paul's."

The Prince's high-profile demands for "traditional" buildings on a human scale and for community involvement in the planning process were developed in his 1988 television documentary, *A Vision of Britain* (and in a 1989 book of the same name). There was an enthusiastic response to his attack on Modernism as an "inhuman" style that had "spawned deformed monsters"; and some equally enthusiastic approval of his praise of the past, his assertion that "We can build new developments which echo the familiar, attractive features of our regional vernacular style."

In 1987, when Prince Charles' views on architecture were being hotly debated in the media in general, West Dorset District Council approached him with a scheme for overspill housing for 5000 people on the edge of Dorchester. The site the Council wanted, a piece of farmland adjoining the western boundary of the town, was owned by the Duchy of Cornwall, and as such was part of the Prince's personal estate; and instead of simply selling the land and allowing developers to put up orthodox residential housing, Prince Charles decided that this was an opportunity to put his principles into practice. Accordingly, in 1988 he commissioned a masterplan for the site from Leon Krier, a Luxembourg-born architect with an

"I would like to see the kinds of materials Wren might have used – soft red brick and stone dressing perhaps, and the ornament and detail of classical architecture, but on a scale humble enough not to compete with the monumentality of St Paul's." THE PRINCE OF WALES

BELOW **The Mies van der Rohe tower (the model is shown here with the developer Peter Palumbo) proposed for a site in the City of London, which was rejected after Prince Charles dismissed it as a "glass stump." Has the Modern Movement "spawned deformed monsters," as the Prince claims?**

established reputation for what has become known as "neotraditionalism." Krier's scheme, in which randomized housing attempts to emulate the slow evolution of the typical English village, was submitted to local residents for comment in 1989; and six years later the first houses, designed by various architects but all in line with the Prince's thinking and the overall code which he and Krier devised for the development, were ready for occupation.

By the time it is finished in 2015, Poundbury will consist of four communities – 3000 homes with their own shops, offices, schools, and other public buildings, grouped around a series of squares and courtyards. To ensure a broad social mix, 20 per cent of the homes are set aside as social housing for rent, with the rest going to owner-occupiers. By spring 1998, the first community was two-thirds of the way to completion.

The first thing to strike the visitor to Poundbury is the variety of housing types and building materials used. In a single square, one can see low rendered cottages with slate roofs and canopied entrances, taller redbrick houses with dormers and bull's-eye windows over the entrance, curving Georgian bays and pilastered white-painted door surrounds. Elsewhere on the estate, cottages faced with golden Cotswold stone stand side by side with houses where rusticated stucco is topped with mellow brick; others still show bands of brick with flint infill. Quotes from the early 18th century, in the shape of "Wrenaissance" red brick walls with stone dressings, painted wooden sashes, and imposing frontispieces, vie with mullioned windows, blue slate roofs, and low tiled porches. There is even an occasional hint of 18th-century Strawberry Hill Gothick, in the pointed arch of a doorway or a narrow lancet window.

And it has to be said that the overall effect is rather attractive. It suggests that the past can provide us with alternatives to the austere Modernist mass-housing developments of the 1950s and 1960s, or the identical rows of boxes that sprang up on the outskirts of so many British towns in the 1970s. Yet it still leaves one with an uneasy feeling.

There are several reasons for this. The first is that Poundbury is a fake – it masquerades as a settlement that evolved during the 18th and 19th centuries and which has been left miraculously unscathed by the theories of Gropius and Le Corbusier and the excesses of their less talented disciples. But its very newness undermines this impression, giving the development a surreal quality. Even when the diggers and portacabins have gone, and time and judicious planting have softened the hard lines of the houses, the carved date-stones over the doorways of the grander houses – "1995," "1996" – will be left as reminders (presumably deliberate) that Poundbury is not, and never can be, what it seems.

The second reason is rooted in the Prince of Wales' attacks on Modernism, of which Poundbury is a direct consequence. There is nothing intrinsically wrong with creating a house, a street, or a whole settlement that looks to the past for its inspiration. All periods, all styles have something to offer. But Poundbury's role as a model for the architecture of the future and, indeed, the

Prince's espousal of Georgian classicism as the only possible style, is every bit as harsh and doctrinaire as a glass stump by Mies van der Rohe. Britain would be a greyer place without such Modernist icons as Berthold Lubetkin's magical Penguin Pool at London Zoo (1934). St Paul's is magnificent, although it neither harmonized with its 17th-century surroundings, nor respected the scale of existing buildings, and would thus have failed the Prince's test of what makes a good building. (One can just imagine the reaction of the cathedral authorities: "A dome? Domes have no place in the tradition of English building.") But the nearby Lloyds' Building (see p.164) is also magnificent. You cannot pick and choose your heritage, any more than you can pick and choose your relatives; tradition is a continuing process, and the individual talent operates within a much wider context than that provided by an 18th-century Dorset town-house or a Greek Revival art gallery.

Ultimately, the argument for a village such as Poundbury – like the Prince of Wales' rejection of Modernist architecture – rests on a single issue: does architecture reflect social values, or does it create them? Will the inhabitants of this brave new world on the outskirts of Dorchester be any less susceptible to the evils that beset late 20th-century society – drug abuse, family breakdown, petty crime, breakfast television – simply because they live in cosy, traditional surroundings?

The estate answers the question, although not perhaps in the way that the Prince of Wales intended. It does indeed reflect current social values. It reflects a lack of confidence in the approaching new century; an isolationist fear of urban life; a yearning to return to a mythical semi-rural Eden in which back doors were left open, neighbours knew each others' names, and children could play in the streets without being molested or stealing car-radios. If only real life were like that.

ABOVE **The Poundbury Enterprise Centre, an exhibition and employment centre with video-conferencing and Internet facilities. The juxtaposition of modern technology and faux-Georgian architecture is vaguely unsettling.**

J. PAUL GETTY AND THE GETTY CENTER

"I'd rather be remembered as an art-collector, not a money-laden businessman." In fact J. Paul Getty is remembered for a lot of things: his staggering wealth and his reluctance to use it (he famously installed a pay-phone for guests in his home); his relentless womanizing; his ill-starred and litigious family. As the 20th century draws to a close, he will also be remembered not so much as an art-collector, more as a man whose money enabled him to buy a certain kind of immortality.

ABOVE **J. Paul Getty (1892–1976), the oil millionaire whose decision to open his Malibu art collection to the public led ultimately to the building of the Getty Center.**

OPPOSITE **The breathtakingly beautiful lobby of the Getty Center (1984–97), the most talked-about building of the decade and the largest cultural complex in the United States.**

The origins of J. Paul Getty's bid for posthumous fame date back to 1931, soon after he became president of the family oil firm. In that year he bought his first significant work of art, a landscape by the 17th-century Dutch painter Jan van Goyen, which cost him $1100 at auction in Berlin. From this beginning – and helped along in the late 1930s by astute purchases in a European art market thrown into panic at the prospect of war – he went on to acquire substantial collections of Dutch, English, and Italian Renaissance paintings, the decorative arts (particularly French tapestries and furniture), and Greek and Roman antiquities. Some were of major international importance, such as the Lansdowne Herakles, a second-century marble figure that he bought for £6000 in the early 1950s and which was to remain one of his favourite pieces.

In 1954 the tax advantages of showing his collections to the public led Getty to open a museum in his ranch house on the Pacific Coast Highway at Malibu in southern California; and 14 years later, as those collections continued to expand, he decided to house them in a brand-new structure built specially for that purpose nearby. His architectural preferences were rooted firmly in the past: "I refuse to pay for one of those concrete-bunker type structures that are the fad among museum architects," he said, "nor for some tinted-glass and stainless-steel monstrosity." Getty's choice of style, however, provoked some raised eyebrows. After toying with the idea of building a faithful replica of Sutton Place, the Tudor mansion in Surrey which was his home from 1960 until his death, he finally opted for an accurate reproduction of an ancient Roman villa. The Villa dei Papiri on the Bay of Naples had been the home of Julius Caesar's father-in-law, Lucius Calpurnius Piso, one of the wealthiest men in the Roman Empire. It was buried in the eruption of Vesuvius in AD 79 that destroyed Herculaneum and Pompeii, and partially excavated by the Swiss engineer Karl Weber in the mid-18th century, before the tunnels which Weber dug filled with gas and then collapsed. Now it was to appear again in all its glory on the coast of California, a bizarre acting-out of Getty's private belief that he had some mystical connection with the Roman emperors, that he was perhaps even the reincarnation of Hadrian.

The critics were not kind when the museum opened in 1974. They described its colonnaded courts, the copies of Pompeian frescoes that decorated its walls, the replicas of bronze statues from the Villa dei Papiri that adorned its gardens, as impossibly vulgar, a Disneyland fantasy, a Cecil B. de Mille set. But the public loved it, and they came in their tens of thousands to see the antiquities and to take a voyeuristic look at the private playground of one of the world's richest men.

Ironically, this was more than Getty himself did. He had left for one of his regular summer business trips to Europe in 1951, and never returned to America. All he ever saw of the remarkable building and the collections it housed was the specially shot movie footage and colour photographs that were regularly dispatched to England, and a scale model of the villa which he would stand and admire for hours at a time.

Just before his death in June 1976, J. Paul Getty added an unexpected codicil to his will, leaving the bulk of his considerable fortune to his museum. This amounted to more than $700 million, and by the time the estate was finally divided in 1982 after a complicated series of family law suits, rising stock prices meant that the endowment totalled some $1.26 billion. At a stroke, the Getty was the wealthiest museum in America. Moreover, because of federal tax laws it was obliged to spend a proportion of its income every year, giving it an annual acquisitions budget of well over $50 million. The inflationary effect this had on the international art market during the 1980s is well known; whatever the Getty wanted, the Getty got, whether it was a Goya for $4 million or a set of Gobelin tapestries for $5.5 million. But the Trustees also decided on new premises for the rapidly escalating collections, which had branched out to include manuscripts, old master drawings, and photographs. In 1982 the Trust bought a spectacular hill-top site in the Santa Monica mountains overlooking Los Angeles. Two years later Richard Meier was chosen as project architect for a 45-hectare (110-acre) campus housing the Museum and various offshoots, including the Getty Conservation Institute, the

Getty Research Institute for the History of Art and the Humanities, the Getty Education Institute for the Arts, and the Getty Grant Program. And in December 1997 the Getty Center, the most talked-about building of the 1990s and the largest cultural complex in the United States, opened its doors to the public.

The complex is tremendously impressive – and uncompromisingly modern, a wry joke at the expense of its dead benefactor's historicist villa in Malibu and his dislike of Modernist architecture. A computerized tram system, giving spectacular views over the surrounding landscape, takes visitors up from the car park to a staircase that in

turn leads to the sweeping asymmetric curves of Meier's buildings, their lower storeys clad in Italian travertine beneath vast expanses of glass and tan aluminium panelling. (Complaints from local residents' associations about reflected glare prevented Meier from using white.) An entrance rotunda gives access to the exhibits, which are contained in five two-storey pavilions grouped around a central court and connected by walkways at both levels. Paintings are housed in skylit galleries, with louvres which adjust automatically to protect their contents. The decorative arts collection is shown in a series of interiors designed by the New York architect Thierry Despont, mixing reconstructed period rooms and genuine panelling with reproduction floor covering, mouldings, and fabrics.

And if the experience of the Center is impressive, so are the statistics on the press release: construction costs of around $1 billion; 10 million man-hours in building time; 40,000 aluminium panels, 230,000 cubic metres (8.1 million cubic feet) of concrete, nearly 300,000 squares of travertine and 15,330 million square metres (165,000 square feet) of exterior glass; 10,000 trees planted in the grounds. Such figures do more than feed our appetite for trivia. They suggest that the Getty

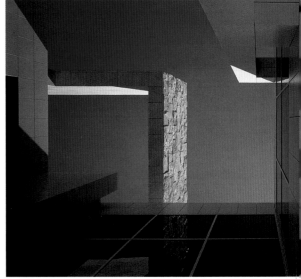

is a monument – and a monument that by sheer force of numbers eclipses the Malibu villa and stands shoulder to shoulder with the great visions of power of the past.

But most impressive of all is the rhetoric. "By the feel and nature of its architecture, the Getty Center embodies permanence," said Harold M. Williams, the President and Chief Executive Officer of the J. Paul Getty Trust. "A return to reality from the land of make-believe," claimed critic Ada Louise Huxtable. "One can come to the Getty Center to see how real kings really lived... nothing is faux." "An oasis for mind and body," wrote Richard Meier. None of these things is true, of course – or at least, they disguise as much as they inform. Beautiful though it is – and it is quite stunningly beautiful – the Getty Center is much too new (and much too close to a faultline) for any talk of permanence. Nor is it a return to reality. A museum is a museum. By its very nature, it holds objects which have been removed from their original setting, divorced from their cultural context, sanitized and conserved and stabilized before being presented for us to admire. Despont's interiors are as faux as a mock-Roman villa on the beach at Malibu simply because they are late 20th- century copies; the function of the genuine furniture and textiles they contain has changed irrevocably by virtue of the fact that they are held up for us to pay homage to the past.

As for being an oasis for mind and body, Meier's remark goes right to the heart of the debate about the Getty Center's symbolism. An oasis implies a surrounding desert, suggesting that Los Angeles (California? America?) is a cultural wilderness that can be watered by European art. Variously compared to a fortified medieval hill-top town and the Acropolis, the Center has been criticized for being separated from the people of Los Angeles, an elitist and exclusionary temple of the arts which is set apart from ordinary mortals and serviced by a priesthood of conserva-

tors and curators, guards and vending machines. Pilgrims climb the hill to worship at the shrine of a Eurocentric high culture that has long since disappeared – and to acknowledge the man who made it all possible, who died 6000 miles away and two decades ago. But what are we admiring as we look at the 18th-century cabinets and the ancient sculpture – taste, or purchasing power, or lost worlds that, even had we lived in them, would have been completely alien to us? In a disposable society, even our visions of power are uncertain.

BELOW **The entrance to the Museum rotunda. Ironically, J. Paul Getty once declared, "I refuse to pay for one of those concrete-bunker type structures that are the fad among museum architects, nor for some tinted-glass and stainless-steel monstrosity."**

BIBLIOGRAPHY

Ackerman, James: *The Architecture of Michelangelo* (London, 1961)

Ackerman, James: *The Villa: Form and Ideology of Country Houses* (London, 1995)

Acton, Harold, and Edward Chaney: *Florence: A Travellers' Companion* (London, 1986)

Adair, John: *The Royal Palaces of Britain* (London, 1981)

Adams, William Howard: *Jefferson's Monticello* (New York, 1983)

Aldred, Cyril: *Akhenaten, King of Egypt* (London, 1988)

Alexander, Michael, ed: *Delhi and Agra: A Travellers' Companion* (New York, 1987)

Anderson, M. S.: *Peter the Great* (London, 1978)

Anisimov, Evgenii V.: *The Reforms of Peter the Great: Progress through Coercion in Russia* (Armonk, New York, 1993)

Baedeker: *Paris* (1996)

Barrucand, Marianne, and Achim Bednorz: *Moorish Architecture in Andalusia* (Munich, 1992)

Baynes, Norman H., ed.: *The Speeches of Adolf Hitler*, 2 vols (Oxford, 1942)

Bazin, Germain: *Baroque and Rococo* (London, 1964)

Begley, W. E., and Z. A. Desai: *Taj Mahal: The Illumined Tomb* (Seattle, 1989)

Bille-De Mot, Eléonore: *The Age of Akhenaten* (Evelyn, Adams & Mackay, 1966)

Blunt, Wilfrid: *The Dream King: Ludwig II of Bavaria* (London, 1970)

Boardman, John, Jasper Griffin and Oswyn Murray, eds: *The Oxford History of the Classical World* (Oxford, 1986)

Boatwright, Mary Taliaferro: *Hadrian and the City of Rome* (Princeton, 1987)

Borsook, Eve: *The Companion Guide to Florence* (London, 1979)

Brown, R. Allen: *Castles, Conquests and Charters* (Woodbridge, 1989)

Brown, R. Allen: *English Castles* (London, 1976)

Browning, Robert: *Justinian and Theodora* (London, 1971)

Burn, Richard, ed.: *The Cambridge History of India: IV, The Mughul Period* (Cambridge, 1937)

Cable, Mary: *El Escorial* (Newsweek, 1971)

Cellini, Benvenuto: *Memoirs* (Oxford, 1928)

Chamberlin, E. R.: *Rome* (New York, 1976)

Chandler, David P.: *A History of Cambodia* (Boulder, 1983)

Clayton, Peter, and Martin Price, eds: *The Seven Wonders of the Ancient World* (London, 1988)

Collier, Richard: *Duce! The Rise and Fall of Benito Mussolini* (London, 1971)

Colvin, H. M., ed.: *The History of the King's Works, vol VI: 1782–1851* (Norwich, 1973)

Cronin, Vincent: *Catherine, Empress of All the Russias* (London, 1978)

Cronin, Vincent: *Louis XIV* (London, 1964)

Cross, Antony, ed.: *Russia Under Western Eyes* (Elek Books, 1971)

Cunliffe, Barry: *Greeks, Romans & Barbarians* (London, 1988)

Davies, Philip: *The Penguin Guide to the Monuments of India* (London, 1989)

Downey, Glanville: *Constantinople in the Age of Justinian* (Norman, Oklahoma, 1960)

Ebrey, Patricia Buckley: *The Cambridge Illustrated History of China* (Cambridge, 1996)

Edwardes, S. M., and H. L. O. Garrett: *Mughal Rule in India* (New Delhi, nd)

Elkins, Stanley, and Eric McKitrick: *The Age of Federalism* (Oxford, 1993)

Etlin, Richard A.: *Modernism in Italian Architecture 1890–1940* (Cambridge, Massachusetts, 1991)

Etter, Roberta Bromley: *Prague* (The Guidebook Company, 1994)

Frampton, Kenneth: *Modern Architecture: a Criticial History* (London, 1980)

Frankfort, Henri: *The Art and Architecture of the Ancient Orient* (London, 1954)

Freeman, Douglas Southall: *George Washington: a Biography* (Eyre and Spottiswoode, 1954)

Fujioka, Michio: *Angkor Wat* (Tokyo, 1972)

Gade, J. A.: *Christian IV* (London, 1928)

Gardiner, Alan: *Egypt of the Pharaohs* (Oxford, 1961)

Gascoigne, Bamber: *The Great Moghuls* (London, 1971)

Girouard, Mark: *Cities and People* (New Haven, 1985)

Gleiniger, Andrea, Gerhard Matzig and Sebastian Redecke: *Paris: Contemporary Architecture* (Munich, 1997)

Grierson, Edward: *King of Two Worlds: Philip II of Spain* (London, 1974)

Hall, John Whitney, ed.: *The Cambridge History of Japan, vol 4 – Early Modern Japan* (Cambridge, 1991)

Hare, Augustus J.: *Walks in Rome* (London, 1903)

Harle, J. C.: *The Art and Architecture of the Indian Subcontinent* (London, 1986)

Harper-Bill, Christopher, Christopher J. Holdsworth and Janet L. Nelson, eds: *Studies in Medieval History* (Woodbridge, 1989)

Haslip, Joan: *Catherine the Great* (London, 1977)

Hempel, Eberhard: *Baroque Art and Architecture in Central Europe* (London, 1965)

Henderson, Bernard W.: *The Life and Principate of the Emperor Hadrian* (London, 1923)

Heydenreich, Ludwig H., and Wolfgang Lotz: *Architecture in Italy: 1400 to 1600* (London, 1974)

Hibbert, Christopher: *George IV, Regent and King* (London, 1973)

Hibbert, Christopher: *The Rise and Fall of the House of Medici* (London, 1979)

Hibbert, Christopher: *Versailles* (Newsweek, 1980)

Hill, Derek, and Lucien Golvin: *Islamic Architecture in North Africa* (London, 1976)

Hilling, John B.: *The Historic Architecture of Wales* (Cardiff, 1976)

Hitler, Adolf: *Hitler's Table Talk, 1941–1944* (Oxford, 1988)

Hoag, John D.: *Islamic Architecture* (London, 1979)

Hochman, Elaine S.: *Architects of Fortune: Mies van der Rohe and the Third Reich* (New York, 1989)

Hollingsworth, Mary: *Patronage in Renaissance Italy* (London, 1994)

Hollingsworth, Mary: *Patronage in Sixteenth-Century Italy* (London, 1996)

Hook, Judith: *Lorenzo de' Medici* (London, 1984)

Hussey, Christopher, and H. Clifford Smith: *Buckingham Palace: Its Furniture, Decoration and History* (London, 1931)

Illik, Drahomir: *The Great Architecture of Japan* (London, 1970)

Irving, Washington: *Treasures of the Alhambra* (Geocolor, 1979)

Jervis, Simon: *Designs for the Dream King: The Castles and Palaces of Ludwig II of Bavaria* (London and New York, 1978)

Kent, John: *Florence and Siena* (London, 1989)

Knecht, R. J.: *Renaissance Warrior and Patron: The Reign of Francis I* (Cambridge, 1994)

Kochan, Miriam: *Life in Russia Under Catherine the Great* (London, 1969)

Kreisel, Heinrich: *Die Schlösser Ludwigs II von Bayern* (Munich, nd)

Lane, Barbara Miller: *Architecture and Politics in Germany 1918–1945* (Cambridge, Massachusetts, 1985)

Lemoine, Pierre: *Versailles: A Guide to the Visit* (Editions d'Art?, nd)

Linderhof Castle – The Official Guide (Bayerische Verwaltung der staatlichen Schlösser, 1965)

Lindsay, Jack: *The Normans and their World* (Purnell, 1974)

Lloyd, Seton, and Hans Wolfgang Müller: *Ancient Architecture* (London, 1980)

Lomax, Derek W.: *The Reconquest of Spain* (Harlow, 1978)

Macadam, Alta: *Blue Guide to Florence* (London, 1995)

Macadam, Alta: *Blue Guide to Rome and its Environs* (London, 1994)

MacDonald, William L.: *The Architecture of the Roman Empire* (New Haven, 1982)

McDonald, Forrest: *The Presidency of George Washington* (Lawrence, Kansas, 1974)

McLaughlin, Jack: *Jefferson and Monticello: the Biography of a Builder* (New York, 1986)

Magnuson, Torgil: *Rome in the Age of Bernini* (Stockholm, 1982)

Mainstone, Rowland J.: *Hagia Sophia: Architecture, Structure and Liturgy of Justinian's Great Church* (London, 1988)

Majumdar, R. C., ed.: *The Mughul Empire* (Bombay, 1974)

Mancini, Giacchino: *Hadrian's Villa and Villa d'Este* (Rome, 1989)

Mark, Robert, and Ahmet Çakmak: *Hagia Sophia from the Age of Justinian to the Present* (Cambridge, 1992)

Mazzeo, Donatello, and Chiara Silvi Antonini: *Monuments of Civilisation: Ancient Cambodia* (London, 1978)

Michell, George: *The Royal Palaces of India* (London, 1994)

Miller, Nory: *Johnson/Burgee: Architecture* (New York, 1979)

Montgomery-Massingberd, Hugh: *Burke's Royal Palaces of Europe* (London, 1984)

Morgan, David: *The Mongols* (Oxford, 1986)

Murnane, William J.: *The Penguin Guide to Ancient Egypt* (London, 1983)

Murray, Linda: *The High Renaissance and Mannerism* (London, 1990)

Neuschwanstein – The Official Guide (Bayerische Verwaltung der staatlichen Schlösser, 1962)

Nicholson, Louise: *The Red Fort, Delhi* (London, 1989)

Ogg, David: *Louis XIV* (Oxford, 1967)

Okawa, Naomi: *Edo Architecture: Katsura and Nikko* (Tokyo, 1975)

Paine, Robert Treat, and Alexander Soper: *The Art and Architecture of Japan*, Pelican History of Art (London, 1955)

Peacocke, Marguerite D.: *The Story of Buckingham Palace* (Odhams, 1951)

Perowne, Stewart: *Hadrian* (Sevenoaks, 1960)

Phillips, E. D.: *The Mongols* (London, 1969)

Pinkney, David H.: *Napoleon III and the Rebuilding of Paris* (Princeton, 1958)

Prestwich, Michael: *Edward I* (London, 1988)

Rachewiltz, I. de: *Papal Envoys to the Great Khans* (London, 1971)

Raeff, Marc: *Understanding Imperial Russia: State and Society in the Old Regime* (New York, 1984)

Redford, Donald B.: *Akhenaten The Heretic King* (Princeton, 1984)

Richards, John F.: *The Mughal Empire* (Cambridge, 1993)

Rodzinski, Witold: *A History of China* (Pergamon, 1979)

Rubin, David Lee, ed.: *Sun King: The Ascendancy of French Culture during the Reign of Louis XIV* (Folger, 1992)

[Friar William of Rubruck]: *The Mission of Friar William of Rubruck* (Hakluyt Society, 1990)

Salvadori, Renzo: *Architect's Guide to Rome* (Oxford, 1990)

Sansom, G. B.: *Japan: A Short Cultural History* (London, 1987)

Saunders, J. J.: *The History of the Mongol Conquests* (London, 1971)

Schmidt, Matthias: *Albert Speer: The End of a Myth* (Edinburgh, 1985)

Schulze, Franz: *Philip Johnson* (New York, 1994)

Sereny, Gitta: *Albert Speer: His Battle with the Truth* (London, 1995)

Seward, Desmond: *Prince of the Renaissance: The Life of François I* (London, 1973)

Shvidkovsky, Dimitri: *The Empress and the Architect: British Architecture and Gardens at the Court of Catherine the Great* (New Haven, 1996)

Sickman, Laurence, and Alexander Soper: *The Art and Architecture of China* (London, 1956)

Siribhadra, Smitthi, and Elizabeth Moore: *Palaces of the Gods: Khmer Art and Architecture in Thailand* (River Books, 1992)

Skovgaard, Joakim: *A King's Architecture: Christian IV and his Buildings* (Hugh Evelyn, 1973)

Smith, Denis Mack: *Mussolini's Roman Empire* (Harlow, 1976)

Smith, W. Stevenson: *The Art and Architecture of Ancient Egypt* (New Haven, 1981)

Snape, Steven: *Egyptian Temples* (Princes Risborough, 1996)

Speer, Albert: *Inside the Third Reich* (London, 1970)

Stewart, Desmond: *The Alhambra* (Newsweek, 1974)

Stierlin, H.: *The Cultural History of Angkor* (Geneva, 1979)

Stoye, John: *Europe Unfolding: 1648–1688* (London, 1988)

Summerson, John: *The Life and Work of John Nash, Architect* (London, 1980)

Sutcliffe, Anthony: *Paris: An Architectural History* (New Haven, 1993)

Taylor, Arnold: *Beaumaris Castle* (Cadw, 1988)

Taylor, Arnold: *Caernarfon Castle and Town Walls* (Cadw, 1989)

Taylor, Arnold: *Harlech Castle* (Cadw, 1988)

Taylor, Arnold: *Studies in Castles and Castle-Building* (London, 1985)

Taylor, Arnold: *The Welsh Castles of Edward I* (London, 1986)

Tillotson, G. H. R.: *Mughal India* (London, 1990)

Troyat, Henri: *Peter the Great* (London, 1987)

Vasari, Giorgio: *The Lives of the Painters, Sculptors and Architects* (Everyman, 1963)

HRH The Prince of Wales: *A Vision of Britain: A Personal View of Architecture* (New York, 1989)

Walton, Guy: *Louis XIV's Versailles* (London, 1986)

Ward, W. H.: *The Architecture of the Renaissance in France* (New York, 1976)

Watkin, David: *The Royal Interiors of Regency England* (J. M. Dent, 1984)

White House Historical Association: *The White House: An Historic Guide* (Washington, 1995)

Wolf, John B.: *Louis XIV* (London, 1968)

Wölfflin, Heinrich: *Renaissance and Baroque* (London, 1964)

Zhuoyun, Yu: *Palaces of the Forbidden City* (London, 1984)

Ziegler, Philip: *King William IV* (London, 1971)

Ziolkowski, John E.: *Classical Influence on the Public Architecture of Washington and Paris* (New York, 1988)

INDEX

Page numbers in *italic* refer to the illustrations

A
Abate, Niccolò dell', 73
Abd al-Hamid Lahori, Shaikh, 99
Aberystwyth Castle, 46, 48
Abu Sa'id, 54
Abu Salim, Sultan of Fez, 54
Abul Fazl, 56, 59
Acqua Vergine, 76
Adams, John, *123*
Adham Khan, 56
Agra, 59, 94–6
Agra Fort, 94–6, 99
Agrippa, Marcus Vipsanius, 22, 76
Akbar the Great, Emperor, 37, 56–9, *56*, 94, *96*, 139
Akhenaten, Pharaoh, 12, 13, 14–19, *14–16*
Akhetaten, 14, 17–19
Alabian, *158*, 160
Albania, 138
Albert, Prince Consort, *112*, 132
Alberti, Leon Battista, *De re aedificatoria*, 62, 68
Alcazaba, Granada, 50
Alexander the Great, 33, 70
Alexandria, 13
Algeria, 37, *37*
Alhambra, Granada, 37, 50–5, *50–5*, 63
Aliotti, Pier Giovanni, 75
All-Union Congress of Soviet Architects, 160
Almohad dynasty, 50
Amarna, 14, 16
Amboise, 70
Amenophis III, Pharaoh, 14
Ammannati, Bartolommeo, 75, 76, *77*
Amun, 14, 16
Angelico, Fra, 64
Angkor Thom, 30
Angkor Wat, 12, 13, 28–33, *28–33*
Anglesey, 46
Anna Catherine of Brandenburg, 90
Anne of Denmark, 90
Anthemius of Tralles, 26, 27
Appollodoros, 20
Aragon, 50, 54, 55

Arc de Triomphe, Paris, 172
Arch of Septimius Severus, Rome, *12*
Ashuruballit I, King of Assyria, 18
AT&T Building, New York, 166–9, *166–9*
Aten, 16–17, 18, 19
Augustus, Emperor, *12*, 20, 22, 37, 147, 150
Aurangzeb, Emperor, 99
Aurelius, Marcus, *71*, 85
Aztecs, 37
B
Ba'albek, 37
Babylon, 13
Baghdad, 42
Balmoral Castle, 132
Bandar Seri Begawan, 174, 176
Barking, 40
Baroque architecture, 85, 88–9, 114
Barshch, Mikhail, 158
Bauhaus, 158
Bavaria, 106, 113, 130–5
Bayeux Tapestry, *38*
Baynards Castle, 40
Beaumaris Castle, 47, *47*
Beijing, 37, 42–5
Belopolski, B., *156*
Bendixen, Siegfried, *112*
Berchet, Federico Pinna, 148
Berger, Jean-Jacques, 144
Berlin, 139, 151, 152–5, *152–5*, 161
Bernini, Gian Lorenzo, 85, 88
Bibliothèque Nationale, Paris, 172, 173
Bismarck, Prince Otto von, *139*
Blair, Tony, 164–5
Blois, 70–1
Blore, Edward, *127*, 129
Bois de Boulogne, 71, 145, 146
Bokassa, Jean-Bedel, 139
Bombay, 37, *37*
Bon, Bartolomeo, *62*
Bormann, Martin, 155
Borneo, 174
Borovikovsky, V., *114*
Borromini, Francesco, 88
Bosch, Hieronymus, 81
Bottai, Giuseppe, 148
Botticelli, Sandro, 64, 68
Bourbon dynasty, 132, 133

Brahe, Tycho, 90, 91
Brahma, 30
Bramante, Donato, 70–1
Brantôme, Pierre, 71, 72, 73
Braunstein, J., 114
Brighton Pavilion, 126
Britain, 113
  Baroque architecture, 89
  Buckingham Palace, 126–9
  Edward I's castles, 46–9
  Norman architecture, 38–41
  Poundbury, 178–81
British Empire, 36, 37
Brock, Thomas, 126, 129
Bronze Age, 12
Brunei, 165, 174–7
Brunelleschi, Filippo, 62, 64, 65–6, *167*, 168
Buckingham, John Sheffield, Duke of, 126
Buckingham Palace, London, 126–9, *127–9*, 164, 165
Buddhism, 30
Builth Castle, 48
Bulfinch, Charles, 124
Burlington, Lord, *Designs of Inigo Jones*, 120
Burma, 42
Bush, John, 116
Byron, Lord, 23
Byzantine Empire, 13, 24–7
C
Caernarfon Castle, 48, 49
Caesar, Julius, 182
Caesar's Palace, Las Vegas, 165
California, 182–5
Cambodia, 28–33
Cameron, Charles, 114–16, *116*, *117*
Canaletto, 62
Capitol, Richmond, Virginia, 121
Capitol, Washington DC, 122, 124
Capri, 134
Carreg Cennen, 46
Carroll, Daniel, 123
Cassel, Richard, 124
Castel Sant'Angelo, Rome, 20, *23*, 77
Castell-y-Bere, 47
Castello, Giovanni Battista, *79*, 80
Castiglione, Baldassare, *Book of the Courtier*, 63
Castile, 50, 53, 54, 55
castles:
  Edward I's castles, 46–9, *47*
  Norman, 39–41

Catherine I, Empress of Russia, 114
Catherine II the Great, Empress of Russia, 113, 114–16, *114*, 143
Catholic Church, 7, 85, 88
  see also Vatican
Catholic League, 90
Cellini, Benvenuto, 70, 81, 168
Central African Republic, 139
Chadwick, Edwin, 145, 147
Chalgrin, Jean-François, 172
Chambord, *63*, 70, 73
Chancellery, Berlin, 8
Changzhou, 42
Chantrey, Sir Francis, 126, 128
Charles, Prince of Wales, 171–2, 178–81, *178*
Charles V, Emperor, 63, 68, 78, 79, 81, *81*
Charles XI, King of Sweden, 106
Charles XII, King of Sweden, 106
Charlotte, Queen of England, 126
chateaux, French Renaissance, 70–3
Cheops, Pharaoh, 12, *13*
Cheshire, 38
Chester, 46, 48
Chevakinsky, Savva, 114
Chicago, 166
China, 42–5, 90
Chingiz (Genghis) Khan, 42
Chitor, 58
Chou li, 44
Christian IV, King of Denmark, 89, 90–3, *90*
Christianity, 26, 50, 74, 84
Chrysler Building, New York, 166, 169
churches:
  Haghia Sophia, Constantinople, 12, 13, 24–7, *24–7*
Circus, Leptis Magna, 37
Cistercians, 48
cities *see* town planning
Classicism, 118, 121, 148
Claude de France, 71
Clement VII, Pope, 68
Clouet, François, *70*
Cockburn, Admiral Sir John, 124, *124*
Coedès, Georges, 32
Colbert, Jean-Baptiste, 105, 106
Colchester Castle, 40

Coleridge, Samuel Taylor, 42
Colosseum, Rome, 84, 150
Colossus of Rhodes, 13
Column of Marcus Aurelius, Rome, 85
Comares Palace, Granada, 53, 54, 55
Commission Supérieure des Monuments Historiques, 170
Compiègne, 71
Coney Island funfair, New York, 165
Confucianism, 44
Conimbriga, 37
Constantine, Emperor, 26
Constantinople, 12, 24–7, 49
Constructivism, 158, 160
Conwy Castle, 48, 49
Copenhagen, 91, 92
Cortés, Hernando, 37
Counter-Reformation, 82
Coysevox, Antoine, *108*, 109
Crete, 12
D
Dafydd ap Gruffydd, 46, 47, 49
Damascus, 42
David, King of Israel, 27
de Gaulle, Charles, 170, 172
deButts, John, 166, 168, 169
Delhi, 94, 96, 97
Denmark, 90–3
Derzhavin, Gavril, 115, *117*
Despont, Thierry, 184, 185
Devon, 38
Diane de Poitiers, *72*
dictators, 139–61
Diderot, Denis, 114
Dimsdale, Thomas, 116
Dio Cassius, 23
Doge's Palace, Venice, *63*
Dollmann, George, 130, 132, 134
Domenico da Cortona, *63*, 71
Dominicans, 66
Donatello, 62, 64, 66
Dorchester, 178, 179
Drake, Francis, 78
Dubarry, Madame, 132
du Cerceau, Jacques Androuet, *72*, 92, 93
Duchy of Cornwall, 179
Dur Sharrukin, 8
Durham, 38
E
Edward I, King of England, 37, 46–9, *46*
Edward II, King of England, 49

Effner, Karl von, 132
Egas, Enrique, 63, 79
Egypt, 12, 13, 14–19, 165
Eleanor of Castile, 49
Elephantine, 19
Elizabeth, Empress of
  Russia, 114
Elizabeth II, Queen of
  England, 164
Ellicott, Andrew, *125*
Empire State Building,
  New York, 166
England *see* Britain
Enlightenment, 113, 115,
  116
Enrique II, King of Castile,
  54
Ephesos, 13
El Escorial, 63, 78–81,
  79–81
Etampes, Duchesse d', 73
Ethiopia, 37
EUR (Esposizione
  Universale di Roma),
  148–51, *149–52*
Fariello, Francesco, 150
Farnese, Ottavio, Duke of
  Parma, *74*
Farnese family, 74
Fascist architecture, 7, 139,
  148–51
Fatehpur Sikri, 56–9, *56–9*,
  94
Ferdinand I, Emperor,
  113, *113*
Fez, 54
Filarete, 63
Il Fiorentino, 70
Flagg, Ernest, 166
Flandrin, Hippolyte, *144*
Flint Castle, 48
Florence, 63, 64–8
Fontainebleau, 71–3, *71–3*
Fontana, Domenico, 82,
  84, 85
Forbidden City, Beijing, 45
Formalism, 160
Fouquet, Nicholas, 104
Fox, Charles James, 116
France:
  Baroque architecture, 89,
    104–9
  grands projets de l'état,
    170–3, *171–3*
  Renaissance, 63, 70–3
  Second Empire, 144–7
Francis I, King of France,
  63, *63*, 70–3, *70*
Fréart de Chambray,
  Parallèle de l'Architecture,
  120
Frederick II, King of
  Denmark, 90, 92

Frederiksborg, *91*, 92–3, *92*
French Revolution, 113, 170
Freud, Sigmund, 14
Functionalism, 160
Garnier, Charles, *147*
Gates, Bill, 174
Gaul, 39
Gautier, Théophile, 50
Géode, La Villette, Paris,
  171, 172
Gelfreikh, 161
George I, King of England,
  6, 89
George III, King of
  England, 126
George IV, King of
  England, 113, 126–9,
  126, 132
Germany, 8, 88, 152–5
Getty, J. Paul, 182–5, *182*
Getty Center, Los Angeles,
  165, 183–5, *183–5*
Getty Center, Malibu,
  182–3, 185
Ghiberti, Lorenzo, 64
Gibbs, James, *Book of
  Architecture,* 120, 124
Gilbert, Cass, 166
Girardon, François, 109
Giscard d'Estaing, Valéry,
  170
Giza, 12, *13*
Go-yozei, Emperor of
  Japan, 100
Gobi Desert, 42
Goebbels, Joseph, 152
Golden House, 112, 113
Golosov, Pantelemon, 158
GoMizuno-o, Emperor,
  100, 102
Göring, Hermann, 152
Goyen, Jan van, 182
Gozzoli, Benozzo, 66, 69
Granada, 37, 50–5, *50–5*
Grande Arche de La
  Défense, Paris, 172, *172*
grands projets de l'état,
  170–3, *171–3*
Great Church,
  Constantinople *see*
  Haghia Sophia
Great Pyramid, Giza, 12,
  13, *13*
El Greco, 81
Gregory XIII, Pope, *62*, 82
Gropius, Walter, 158, 159,
  160, 180
Grüner, Ludwig, 164
Guaranty Building,
  Buffalo, New York, 168
Gudden, Bernard von, 135
Guerrini, *149*, 150
Guicciardini, Francesco, 67

Gundulf, Bishop of
  Rochester, 40
Hadrian, Emperor, 12, 13,
  20, *20*, 27, 68, 85, 182
Haghia Sophia,
  Constantinople, 12, 13,
  24–7, *24–7, 132*
Halicarnassus, 13
Hampton Court, 89, 106
Hanging Gardens of
  Babylon, 13
Hangzhou, 42
Hanover, Elector of, 106
Hardouin-Mansart, Jules,
  105–6
Haremhab, Pharaoh, 19
Harlech Castle, *47*, 48, *49*
Harold II, King of
  England, 38
Hassanal Bolkiah, Sultan
  of Brunei, 165, 174–7,
  174
Hastings, 39
Hastings, Battle of (1066),
  38
Haussmann, Georges,
  144–7, *145*
Hawarden Castle, 46
Henry II, King of France,
  72, 73
Henry VII, King of
  England, 63
Henry VIII, King of
  England, 63
Herculaneum, 182
Herrenchiemsee, 106, 130,
  133–4
Herrera, Juan de, 80
Het Loo, 106
Hideyoshi, Toyotomi, 100
Himmler, Heinrich, 155
Hinduism, 30, 32, 58
Hiroshima, 38
Hitler, Adolf, 8, 139, *139*,
  148, 150, 151, 152–5,
  152, 158, 161
Hoban, James, *123*, 124
Hohenschwangau, 130
Holy Roman Empire, 79
Home Insurance Building,
  Chicago, 166
Hôtel de Salm, Paris, 119
Hotel Moskva, Moscow, 161
House of the Sun-disc, Tell
  El-Amarna, 13, 18
humanism, 63
Humayun, Emperor, 56, 98
Hume, Joseph, 128
Huxtable, Ada Louise, 185
Ille, Eduard, *132*
Inayat Khan, 96
Incas, 37

India, 37, 56–9, 94–9
India Gate, New Delhi, *8*
Indo-China, 42
Inquisition, 78, 82
Institut du Monde Arabe,
  Paris, *171*, 172
International Style, 166
Iofan, Boris, *157*, 159, 160
Iraq, 8
Ireland, 38
Irving, Washington, 50
Isaacs, Pieter, *90*
Isabella of Portugal, 78
Isidorus of Miletus, 26, *27*
Islam, 55, 58, 59
Ismâ'il, 54
Istana Nurul Iman, 174–7,
  175–7
Italy:
  Baroque architecture, 88
  Fascist architecture,
    148–51
  Renaissance, 63, 64–8,
    74–7, 82–5
Jahangir, Emperor, 94
Jame' Asr Hassanal
  Bolkiah Mosque, Bandar
  Seri Begawan, 176
James I, King of England,
  89, 90
James of St George, 48
Jank, Christian, 130, 134
Japan, 42, 100–4
Java, 42
Jayavarman IV, King, 30
Jayavarman VI, King, 28
Jefferson, Thomas, 7, 113,
  118–21, *118*, 122–3, 124,
  125
Jenney, William Le Baron,
  166
Jesuits, 58
Jews, 33
Johnson, Philip, *9*, 166–9,
  166–9
Jones, Inigo, 89, 120
Juan Bautista da Toledo,
  78, *79*, 80
Julius III, Pope, 74–7, *74*, 82
Jurchens, 42, 45
Justinian, Emperor, 12, 13,
  24–7, *24*
Jutland, 91
Karakorum, 42
Karnak, 14, 16, 19
Kashmir, 59
Katsura Imperial Villa,
  100–4, *101–4*
Kent, 38
Kent, William, *Designs of
  Inigo Jones,* 120
Khmer Empire, 12, 13,

28–33
Khmer Rouge, 28
Khruschev, Nikita, 160
Kim Il Sung, 139
Knossos, 12
Koldinghus, 91
Koran, 54, 58, 98
Krier, Leon, 179–80, *179*
Krishna, 32
Kuala Lumpur, 166
Kubilai Khan, 37, 42–5, *42*,
  139
Kumsusan Memorial
  Palace, Pyongyang, 139
Kunstkamera, St
  Petersburg, 142
Kyoto, 102
La Défense, Paris, 172
La Fosse, Charles de, 109
La Padula, *149*, 150
La Rochefoucauld-
  Liancourt, Duc de, 119,
  120
La Turbie, 37
Lamb, William, 166
Las Vegas, 165
Latrobe, Benjamin, *123*,
  124
Laurentinum, 76
Lawrence, Sir Thomas, *126*
Le Breton, Gilles, *71*, 72, 73
Le Brun, Charles, 105,
  107, 109
Le Corbusier, 158, 159,
  160, 166, 180
Le Nôtre, André, 105
Le Roy, Philibert, 104
Le Vau, Louis, 105
Lebanon, 37
Leblond, Jean-Baptiste
  Alexandre, *143*
Leinster House, Dublin, 124
L'Enfant, Pierre Charles,
  122, 123, 124, 125
Lenin, *139*, 156, 160
Leonardo da Vinci, 63, 68,
  70, 71
Leoni, Giacomo, *6*
Leoni, Leone, 81
Leoni, Pompeo, 81
Leopold III, Emperor, 106
Leptis Magna, 37
Libera, Adalberto, 149,
  150, *150*
Libya, 37
Lincoln, 40
Linderhof, 130, 132, *133*,
  134, *135*
Lippert, Julius, 152
Liverpool, Lord, 126, 127
Llandovery, 46
Lloyds' Building, London,
  164, 165, 181

Llywelyn ap Gruffydd, 46–7, 49
Lomonosov, Mikhail, 116
London, 40–1, 122, 126–9, 178, *180*
Longman, Evelyn, 168
Lorca, Federico Garcia, 50
Los Angeles, 183–5
Louis XIII, King of France, 105, 106, 133
Louis XIV, King of France, 89, *89*, 104–9, *104*, 132, 133, 173
Louis XV, King of France, 73, 132, *133*, 134
Louis XVI, King of France, 132
Louis Philippe, King of France, 113
Louvre, Paris, 71, 145, 170–2, *173*
Low Countries, 88
Lubetkin, Berthold, 181
Ludwig I, King of Bavaria, 113
Ludwig II, King of Bavaria, 106, 113, 130–5, *130*, 155
Lutyens, Edwin, 7, 8, 168
Luxor, 14
Luxor Las Vegas, *164–5*

M
Mabinogion, 48, 49
Machiavelli, Niccolò, *The Prince*, 63
Mächler, Martin, 152
Madrid, 78
Maison Carré, Nîmes, 121
Makramat Khan, 97
Malaysia, 166, 174
Malibu, 182–3, 185
Malkata, 14
Mannerism, 73
Mansion House, London, 178
Marble Arch, London, 126, 127–8, *127*, 129
Marie-Antoinette, Queen of France, 103, 132
Marinid dynasty, 53, 54
Marsy brothers, 108
Mary II, Queen of England, 89
Mary Tudor, Queen of England, 70, 78, 81
Masaccio, 62
Mattarnovy, Georg-Iohann, 142
Mausoleum, Halicarnassus, 13
Maxen, Emperor, 48, 49
Maximilian II, King of Bavaria, 113, 132
Mazarin, Cardinal, 104
Medici, Alessandro de',

Duke of Florence, 68
Medici, Cosimo de' the Elder, 64–7, *64*, 68, *69*
Medici, Giovanni de', 68
Medici, Giovanni di Bicci de', 64
Medici, Giuliano de', 68
Medici, Lorenzo the Magnificent, 67–8, *69*, 71
Medici, Piero the Gouty, 67
Medici family, 63, 64–8
Meier, Richard, 183–4, *184*, 185
Melnikov, Konstantin, 158
Memphis, 14, 19
Mexico, 37
Meyer, Hannes, 158
Michelangelo, 23, 63, *67*, 68, 74, 75, 76, 83, *84*
Michelozzo di Bartolomeo, 64, 66, *66*, 67
Michelucci, Giovanni, 149
Mies van der Rohe, Ludwig, *9*, 166, 178, *180*, 181
Milan, 79
Milan, Dukes of, 63
Millennium Dome, Greenwich, 164–5
Ming dynasty, 45
Minkus, 161
Minoan culture, 12
Mir Abd al-Karim, 97
Mitterrand, François, 165, 170–3, *170*
Modernism, 149, 158, 160, 166–8, 178, 180–1, 184
Moghul Empire, 7, 37, 56–9, 88, 89, 94–9
Molière, 104
Mongols, 42–5
Monte Carlo, 37
Montez, Lola, 113
Montgomery, Treaty of (1267), 46
Monticello, 118–21, *119–20*
Moore, Mr, 118
Moore, Thomas, 123, 124
Moorish architecture, 50–5, *50–5*
Moretti, Luigi, 150
Moron, Eleanor, 32
Morris, Robert, *Select Architecture*, 120
Moscow, 140–1, 143, 155, 156–61, *157–9*, *161*
Moscow Metro, 160–1
Moscow University, 161, *161*
Moses, 14
Moskva Hotel, Moscow, 156, *159*
motte-and-bailey, 39–40
Mouhaut, Henri, 32
Mount Meru, *29*, 30, 31, 33

Mouridsen family, 93
Muhammad, Prophet, 59
Muhammad I, Sultan, 50–3
Muhammad II, Sultan, 50–3
Muhammad V, Sultan, 50–5, *52*
Mumtaz Mahal, *94*, 97, 98
Munich, 134
Muratori, Saverio, 150
Mussolini, Benito, 37, 139, 148–51, *148*
Muzio, Giovanni, 149

N
Nanjing, 45
Naples, 63, 78
Napoleon I, Emperor, 144, 146, 171
Napoleon III, Emperor, 130, 132, 139, 144–7, *144*, 173
Nash, John, 126, 127–9, *127*, 129
Nasrid dynasty, 50–5
National Gallery, London, 178
Nattier, Jean-Marc, *140*
Nazis, 150, 152–5, *154*
Neferkheperuhersekheper, *19*
Nefertiti, Queen, *16*, 17–18, 19
neoclassicism, 120, 121, 125, 160
neo-Palladianism, 120
neo-traditionalism, 180
Nero, Emperor, 112, 113
Netherlands, 106, 109
Neuschwanstein, 113, 130–2, *131–2*, 133, 134
New Delhi, 7, 8
New York, 165, 166–9, *167–9*
Nicholas V, Pope, 64, 83
Nienschanz, 140
Nile, River, 16
Nizam ud din Ahmad Bakshi, 96
Nocret, Jean, *104*, 109
Noritada, Prince, 100, *102*, 102
Normans, 36, 38–41, 44, 47–8
North America, 36
North Korea, 139
Nöteborg, 140
Nouvel, Jean, *171*, 172
Novecento Movement, 150
Nuremberg, 153, *154*

O
Olympia, 13
Omar Ai Saifuddien III, Sultan of Brunei, 174, 176
Opéra de la Bastille, Paris,

172–3
Opéra Garnier, Paris, 145, *147*, 173
Organization of the Union of Soviet Architects, 158
Osiris, 16
Ospedale degli Innocenti, Florence, 65
Oswestry, 46
Ott, Carlos, 173

P
Paciotta, Francesco, *79*, 80
Palace of the Soviets, Moscow, *157*, 158–60
Palace of the Tuileries, Paris, *89*
palaces:
  Alhambra, Granada, 50–5, *50–5*
  Buckingham Palace, London, 126–9, *127–9*, 164, 165
  El Escorial, 63, 78–81, *79–81*
  Fatehpur Sikri, 56–9, *56–9*, 94
  Fontainebleau, 71–3, *71–3*
  Frederiksborg, *91*, 92–3, 92
  Istana Nurul Iman, 174–7, *175–7*
  Katsura Imperial Villa, 100–4, *101–4*
  Neuschwanstein, 113, 130–2, *131–2*, 133, 134
  Palazzo Medici, Florence, 64, 66–8, *66*, 69
  Renaissance, 66–8, *66–8*
  Tsarskoye Selo, 113, 114–16, *114–17*
  Versailles, 85, 89, 104–9, *104–9*, 122, 125, 132, 133, 143, 153
Palazze dell'Esposizioni, EUR, *151*
Palazzo dei Congressi, EUR, 150, *150*
Palazzo del Quirinale, Rome, 62
Palazzo della Civiltà Italiana, EUR, *149*, 150–1
Palazzo Medici, Florence, 64, 66–8, *66*, 69
Palladianism, 124, 125
Palladio, Andrea, 118, 120, 121
  Quattro Libri dell'Architettura, 6, *6*, 120
Palmyra, 37
Palumbo, Peter, *180*
Paniconi, Mario, 149
Pantheon, Rome, 12, 13, *21*, 22–3, *22*, 27, 62, 68
Paris, 119, 144–7, *145–7*,

170–3, *171–3*
Paul III, Pope, 74
Paul Petrovich, Grand Duke, 116, *116*
Paul the Silentiary, 26
Peacock Throne, 96, 97
Peale, Charles Wilson, *122*
Pearl Mosque, Agra, 94
Pearse, Padraic, 38
Pediconi, Giulio, 149
Pedro I, King of Castile, 54
Pei, I.M., 170–2, *173*
Pelli, Cesar, 166
Penguin Pool, London Zoo, 181
Pennethorne, Sir James, 164
Perrault, Dominique, 172
Persigny, 144
Peru, 37
Peter, St, 85
Peter III, Tsar, 114
Peter and Paul Fortress, St Petersburg, 141, *141*, *142*
Peter the Great, Tsar, 91, 106, 114, 139, 140–3, *140*, 161
Peterhof, 106, *143*
Petit Trianon, Versailles, 132
Petrarch, 62
Petrie, Sir Flinders, 14
Petronas Towers, Kuala Lumpur, 166
Pevensey, 39
Pharos of Alexandria, 13
Philip II, King of Spain, 78–81, *78*, 88
Phnom Penh, 28
Piacentini, Marcello, 148, 149, 150, 151
Piazza Imperiale, EUR, 150
Piazza of St Peter's, Rome, 88
Pierrefonds, 130, 132
Pinochet, Augusto, 139
Piso, Lucius Calpurnius, 182
Pius II, Pope, 64, *64*
Pius IX, Pope, 113
Pizarro, Francisco, 37
Pliny the Younger, 76
Poggio a Caiano, 71
Pol Pot, 139
Polo, Marco, 42, 44, 45, *45*
Polo, Niccolo, *45*
Pompeii, 182
Pompidou, Georges, 170
Ponti, Gio, 150–1
Pontormo, Jacopo, *64*
Porta, Giacomo della, 83
Portugal, 37
Postmodernism, 169, 178
Poundbury, Dorset,

178–81, *179–81*
Prague Castle, 113, *113*
Primaticcio, Francesco, 70, 72–3, *73*
Procopius of Caesarea, *26*, 27
The Secret History, 24, 27
Punjab, 59
Pyongyang, *138*, 139
pyramids, Egypt, 12

Q
Quaroni, Ludovico, 150

R
Racine, 114
Rajputs, 58
Rama, 30
Rastrelli, Bartolomeo, 114, *115*
Rationalism, 148–9, 150, 168
Red Army Theatre, Moscow, *158*, 160
Red Fort, Delhi, 94, 96–7, *97*, 99
Redwan, Vizir, 54
Renaissance, 62–85
Rhuddlan, battle of (1282), 47
Rhuddlan Castle, 48, 49
Ricci, Sebastiano, 6
Richardt, Ferdinand, *91*
Riedel, Edward, 130
Rochester Cathedral, 40
Rogers, Richard, *164*, 165
Roman Empire, 12, 13, 20–3, 24, 26, 37, *37*, 44, 148, 165, 182
Romanesque architecture, 131
Romania, 138
Romano, *149*, 150
Rome, 12, *12*, 20–3, 27, 62, *62*, 74–7, 80, 82–5, *83*, 118, 125, 147, 148–51, *149–51*
Rosenborg, 93, *93*
Roskilde Cathedral, 91–2
Rosso (Il Fiorentino), 72, 73, *73*
Rousseau, Jean Jacques, 114
Rousseau, Pierre, 119
Royal Institute of British Architects, 178
Rubens, Peter Paul, *78*
Rudnev, 161
Russia, 7, 113, 114–16, 140–3, 155

S
Saint-Germain-en-Laye, 71
St James's Palace, London, 126
St John Lateran, Rome, 83, 85
St Paul's Cathedral,

London, 178, 181
St Peter's, Rome, *7*, 74, 78, 82, 83, 84, *84*
St Petersburg, 125, 140–3, *141–2*, 156, 161
St Quentin, battle of (1557), 78
Salim, Shaikh, 56, 57, *59*
San Carlo alla Quattro Fontane, Rome, 88
San Lorenzo, Florence, 65, *67*, 68
San Marco, Florence, 66
San Pietro in Monterio, Rome, 74
Sangallo, Giuliano da, 71
Santa Croce, Florence, 168
Santa Maria Maggiore, Rome, *84*, 85
Santa Maria Novella railway station, Florence, 149
Santa Monica, 183
Santiago de Compostela, 63, 79
Santo Domingo, San Cristobal, *36*
Sarawak, 174
Sargon II, King of Assyria, 8
Sarto, Andrea del, 70
Savonarola, Girolamo, 68
Saxons, 38, 39
Schachinger, Gabriel, *130*
Schleswig-Holstein, Countess Kirsten von, 90
Schloss Berg, 134–5
Schloss Schachen, 134
Schönbrunn, 106
Scudéry, Madeleine de, 109
Seagram Building, New York, *9*, 165, 166
Serlio, Sebastiano, 70, 72, 92
Seven Wonders of the World, 12, 13, *13*
Severus, Septimius, Emperor, *12*, 84
Shah Jahan, 89, 94–9, *94*
Shahjahanabad, 96, *97*, *98*, 99
Shang-tu, 42
Shchusev, Aleksei, 156, 159, *159*, 160
Shell, 174
Shelley, Percy Bysshe, 8, 23
Sher Shah, 98
Shrewsbury, 46
Shropshire, 38
Signoria, 64, 68
Sigüenza, José de, 80
Silchester, 37
Simbirtsev, *158*, 160
Singer Tower, New York, 166

Siniavskii, Mikhail, 158
Sistine Chapel, Vatican, 74
Siva, 30
Sixtus V, Pope, 82–5, *82*, *84*
skyscrapers, 166–9, *166–9*
Smenkhkare, Pharaoh, 18
Snowdonia, 46, 47
socialist realism, 160
Solomon, King of Israel, 27
Sony Corporation, 169
Soviet Union, 156–61
Spain, 37, 88
  Moorish architecture, 50–5, *50–5*
  Renaissance, 63, 78–81
Spartianus, Aelius, 22
Speer, Albert, 139, 152–5, *152–5*
Spreckelsen, Johann Otto von, 172, *172*
Staffordshire, 38
Stalin, Joseph, 7, 139, 148, 155, 156–61, *156*
Stalinism, 138
Steenwinckel, Hans van the elder, *91*
Steenwinckel, Hans van the younger, 93, *93*
Stendhal, 23, 72
Stevens, F.W., 37, *37*
Stowe, 116
Sullivan, Louis, 168
Summer Palace, St Petersburg, 141
Sung Empire, 42
Suryavarman II, King, 12, 13, 28–33, *28*
Sutton Place, Surrey, 182
Sweden, 90, 93, 140

T
Ta-tu, 42, *43*, 44–5
Taj Mahal, 94, *95*, 96–9, *99*
Tatlin, Vladimir, 158
Tell El-Amarna, 12
temples:
  Angkor Wat, 28–33, *28–33*
  Temple of Artemis, Ephesos, 13
  Temple of Venus and Rome, 20
Thebes, 14, 16, 17, 18
Theodora, Empress, 24, 27
Thirty Years War, 88, 90
Thornton, Dr William, 124, *125*
Thuringia, 130
Timgad, 37, *37*
Titian, 81
Tokugawa Kazuko, 100
Tokugawa shoguns, 100
Torrigiani, Pietro, 63
Toshihito, Prince, 89, 100–4

Tower of London, *39–41*, 40–1
town planning:
  Berlin, 151, 152–5, *152–5*
  Moscow, 155, 156–61, *157–9*, 161
  Paris, 144–7, *145–7*
  Rome, 148–51, *149–51*
  St Petersburg, 125, 140–3, *141–2*, 156, 161
  Washington DC, 121, 122–5, *123–5*
Trajan, Emperor, 20, 22, 33
Trajan's Column, Rome, 85
Trezzini, Domenico, 141–2, *141*
Tropaeum Alpinum, La Turbie, 37
Tsarskoye Selo, 113, 114–16, *114–17*
Tuby, Jean-Baptist, 108, *109*
Tuscany, Grand Dukes of, 68
Tutankhamun, Pharaoh, 18–19, 170
Tuthmosis, 14
Tytler, Alexander, 64

U
Uffizi Palace, Florence, *65*
United States of America, 118–21, 122–5, 166–9, 182–5
University of Virginia, Charlottesville, 121, *121*
Ustad Ahmad, 97–8
Ustad Isa Afandi, 97
Uttar Pradesh, 59

V
van Alen, William, 166
Vasari, Giorgio, 68, 74–5, 76
  Lives of the Artists, 75
Vatican, 71, 77, 83, *85*
Vaux-le-Vicomte, 104, 105
Venice, 63, *63*
Venturi, Robert, 178
Versailles, 85, 89, 104–9, *104–9*, 122, 125, 132, 133, 143, 153
Vesnin brothers, 158
Vesuvius, Mount, 182
Victoria, Queen of England, *112*, 132
Victoria Memorial, London, 126, 129
Victoria Railway Terminus, Bombay, 37, *37*
Vignola, Giacomo Barozzi da, 70, 75–6, *75*

Vignola, Jacopo, 92
Villa Adriana, Rome, 20
Villa dei Papiri, Naples, 182–3
Villa Giulia, Rome, 74–7, 75–7
Villa Pisani, 118
Villers-Cotterêts, 71
Vilnius, *139*
Viollet-le-Duc, Eugène, 130
Vishnu, 30, 31, 32, 33
Voltaire, 114, 116
Vries, Adrian de, 93
Vries, Hans Vredeman de, 92

W
Wagner, Richard, 130, 133
Wales, 46–9
Wallingford, 38
War Memorial Arch, New Delhi, *7*, *8*
Wartburg, 130, 131
Washington, George, 113, 118–19, *122*, 125
Washington DC, 121, 122–5, *123–5*
Webb, Sir Aston, 126, *127*, 129, *129*
Weber, Friedrich, 143
Weber, Karl, 182
Westminster, 46
Westminster Abbey, London, 63
White Tower, Tower of London, *39–41*, 40–1
Wilkins, William, 178
William I, King of England, 37, 38–41, *38*
William III, King of England, 89, 106
William IV, King of England, *127*, 129
William of Poitiers, 40
William Rufus, King of England, 41
Williams, Harold M., 185
Winchester, 46
Windsor Castle, *112*, 126, 132
Woolworth Building, New York, 166, 169
Worcester, 46
Wren, Christopher, 7, 85, 89, 122, 178
Wright, Frank Lloyd, 160

Y
Yasodharapura, 30, 32
Yasovarman I, King, 30
York, 38, 40
Yûsuf I, Sultan, *51*, 53, 55
Yuan dynasty, 42–5

Z
Zeus, statue of, 13
Zhu Yuanzhang, 45

AUTHOR'S ACKNOWLEDGMENTS

I owe a special debt of gratitude to the following: Lucas Dietrich, who has such good ideas; Anthony Beeson and Ian Osborn of the late and much-lamented Bristol Art Library, without whose erudition and unfailing good humour this project wouldn't have been half as much fun; Elisabeth Faber and Alison Starling, whose patience and understanding were more than any author has a right to expect; staff at the London Library and the various libraries of Bristol University; and, last but never least, Helen. To them, and to everyone else who has made this book possible, thanks.

PICTURE CREDITS

The publisher would like to thank the following for their kind permission to reproduce photographs for use in this book.

Key b bottom, **l** left, **r** right, **t** top

Front jacket Topham Picturepoint
Back jacket Richard Payne/Philip Johnson & John Burgee in association with Henry Simmons
1 Richard Payne/Philip Johnson & John Burgee in association with Henry Simmons; **2–3** Image Bank/Grant V Faint; **6** British Library/Shelf mark: 557; **7** E.T. Archive/Ca Rezzonico Museum, Venice; **8** Topham Picturepoint; **9** Corbis UK Ltd/Angelo Hornak; **10** Image Bank/Navada Wier **12** Werner Forman Archive **13** Getty Images/Stephen Studd; **14** AKG, London/SMPK, Egyptisches Museum, Berlin; **15** AKG, London/National Museum, Cairo; **16** Werner Forman Archive/Schimmel Collection, New York; **17** Werner Forman Archive/El-Minya Museum, Egypt; **19** Davies, N de G, The Rock Tombs of El-Amarna, 1908, pl xliii; **20** Topham Picturepoint **21** AKG, London; **22** Ancient Art and Architecture Collection/Ronald Sheridan; **23** Getty Images/Oliver Benn; **24** Robert Harding Picture Library/JHC Wilson; **25** Image Bank/Carlos Navajas; **26 t** Werner Forman Archive, **b** Robert Harding Picture Library; **27** Robert Harding Picture Library/Adam Woolfitt; **28** Ancient Art and Architecture Collection/B Crisp; **29** Robert Harding Picture Library/Tim Hall; **30** AKG, London/Henning Bock; **31** Corbis UK Ltd/Wolfgang Kaehler; **33** Ancient Art and Architecture Collection/B Crisp; **34–5** Robert Harding Picture Library/Ruth Tomlinson; **36** Robert Harding Picture Library/Chris Rennie; **37 t** Robert Harding Picture Library/Adam Woolfitt, **b** Robert Harding Picture Library/JHC Wilson; **38** Ancient Art and Architecture Collection/Ronald Sheridan; **39** Robert Harding Picture Library/Walter Rawlings; **40** Topham Picturepoint; **41** Robert Harding Picture Library/Adam Woolfitt; **42** AKG, London; **43** Bridgeman Art Library, London/New York/Private Collection; **45** AKG, London/Bibliotheque Nationale, Paris; **46** Topham Picturepoint/British Museum; **47** Robert Harding Picture Library; **48** Ancient Art and Architecture Collection/Cheryl Hogue; **49** Ancient Art and Architecture Collection/Ronald Sheridan; **50** Getty Images/John Lawrence; **51** Werner Forman Archive; **52** Robert Harding Picture Library/Nedra Westwater; **53** Robert Harding Picture Library/Adam Woolfitt; **55** Werner Forman Archive; **56** Victoria & Albert Museum; **57** Link Picture Library/Orde Eliason; **58** Link Picture Library/Orde Eliason; **59** Link Picture Library/Orde Eliason; **60–61** Robert Harding Picture Library/Roy Rainford; **62** Bridgeman Art Library, London/New York/Christie's Images; **63 t** Getty Images/Chris Haigh, **b** Ancient Art and Architecture Collection/Ronald Sheridan; **64** AKG, London/Erich Lessing; **65** Corbis UK Ltd/Robert Holmes; **66** Scala; **67** Getty Images/Simeone Huber; **69** Scala; **70** AKG, London/Musee du Louvre, Paris/Erich Lessing; **71** Robert Harding Picture Library/Nedra Westwater; **72 l** Corbis UK Ltd/Paul Almsley, **r** Corbis UK Ltd/Robert Holmes; **73** Robert Harding Picture Library/P Tetrel; **74** Scala/Palazzo Farnese, Caprarola; **75** Scala/Villa Giulia Roma; **76** Scala/Villa Giulia Roma; **77** Corbis UK Ltd/John Heseltine; **78** Bridgeman Art Library, London/New York/Museo del Prado, Madrid/Index; **79** AKG, London; **80** Robert Harding Picture Library/Robert Frerck/Odyssey/Chicago; **81** Robert Harding Picture Library/Adam Woolfitt; **82** AKG, London; **83** AKG, London/Vatican Rome; **84 l** Corbis UK Ltd/John Hesletine, **r** Robert Harding Picture Library; **85** Scala/Biblioteca Vaticana; **86–7** Werner Forman Archive; **88** Bridgeman Art Library, London/New York/British Library, London; **89** Bridgeman Art Library, London/New York/Chateau de Versailles; **90** AKG, London; **91** Bridgeman Art Library, London/New York/Christie's Images; **92** E.T. Archive; **93** Danish Tourist Board/Soren Jensen; **94** Bridgeman Art Library, London/New York/Private Collection; **95** Topham Picturepoint; **96** Robert Harding Picture Library/Adam Woolfitt; **97** Corbis UK Ltd/Chris Hellier; **98** Corbis UK Ltd/Sheldan Collins; **99** Getty Images/Nicholas DeVore; **100** Arcaid/Bill Tingey; **101** Corbis UK Ltd/Robert Holmes; **102** Corbis UK Ltd/Sakamoto Photo Research Laboratory; **103** Corbis UK Ltd/Sakamoto Photo Research Laboratory; **104** Bridgeman Art Library, London/New York/Chateau de Versailles, France/Giraudon; **105** Bridgeman Art Library, London/New York/Chateaux de Versailles, France/Giraudon; **106** Getty Images; **107** AKG, London/Erich Lessing; **108** Bridgeman Art Library, London/New York/Chateau de Versailles, France 109** Image Bank/Carlos Navajas; **110–11** AKG, London; **112** Bridgeman Art Library, London/New York/British Library, London; **113** Russia & Republics Photolibrary/Mark Wadlow; **114** Novosti; **115** Bridgeman Art Library, London/New York/Tsarskoye Selo, Moscow, Russia; **116 l** Bridgeman Art Library, London/New York/Tsarskoye Selo, Moscow, Russia, **r** Russia & Republics Photolibrary/Mark Wadlow; **117** Bridgeman Art Library, London/New York/Tsaskoye Selo, Moscow, Russia; **118** Bridgeman Art Library, London/New York/Pennsylvania Academy of Fine Arts, Philadelphia; **119** AKG, London; **120** Image Bank/Mercury Archives **121 t** The Architect of the Capitol/National Graphic Center, Virginia, **b** Corbis/Library of Congress; **122** Corbis-Bettmann; **123** Corbis UK Ltd/Buddy Mays; **124** Corbis UK Ltd/Buddy Mays; **125** Topham Picturepoint/John Baker; **126** Bridgeman Art Library, London/New York/National Gallery of Ireland, Dublin; **127** Illustrated London News Picture Library; **128** Museum of London; **129** Robert Harding Picture Library/Mark Mawson; **130** AKG, London; **131** Barnabys Picture library/O J Troisfontaines; **132** AKG, London; **133** Robert Harding Picture Library/Dave Jacobs; **135** Topham Picturepoint; **136–7** AKG, London; **138** Topham Picturepoint; **139 t** Rex Features/East News-Sipa Press, **b** AKG, London; **140** Bridgeman Art Library, London/New York/Hermitage, St Petersburg; **141** Barnabys Picture library; **142** AKG, London; **143** AKG, London; **144** Bridgeman Art Library, London/New York/Chateau de Versailles, France/Lauros-Giraudon; **145** Jean-Loup Charmet; **146** Jean-Loup Charmet; **147** AKG, London; **148** Topham Picturepoint; **149** AKG, London/Hilbich; **150** Corbis UK Ltd/David Lees; **151** Corbis UK Ltd/Franz-Marc Frei; **152** Getty Images; **153** AKG, London; **154** AKG, London; **155** AKG, London; **156** AKG, London; **157** AKG, London; **158** Society for Cooperation in Russian & Soviet Studies; **159** Novosti; **161** Corbis UK Ltd/Michael S Yamashita; **162–3** Robert Harding Picture Library/Bud Freund; **164** Getty Images/Janet Gill; **165** Getty Images/Tony Craddock; **166** Topham Picturepoint; **167** Angelo Hornak/Philip Johnson & John Burgee in association with Henry Simmons; **168** Richard Payne, FAIA/Philip Johnson & John Burgee in association with Henry Simmons; **169** Angelo Hornak/Philip Johnson & John Burgee in association with Henry Simmons; **170** Topham Picturepoint; **171 t** Image Bank/Thierry Boisson, **b** Robert Harding Picture Library/C Martin; **172** Robert Harding Picture Library/Nigel Francis; **173** Popperfoto/Michelangelo Gratton; **174** Camera Press/Rota; **175** Camera Press/John Shelley; **176 top** Camera Press/John Shelley, **b** Robert Harding Picture Library/Gavin Hellier; **177** Camera Press/Alan Whicker; **178** Rex Features/Tim Rooke; **179 t** Arcaid/Percy Thomas Ptrs/Joe Low; **b** Rex Features; **180** Topham Picturepoint; **181** Rex Features/Tim Rooke; **182** Camera Press/Ian Bodenham; **183** The Getty Center/The J Paul Getty Trust/Alex Vertikoff; **184 l** Arcaid/John Edward Linden/Richard Meier, **r** Arcaid/John Edward Linden/Architect: Richard Meier; **185** Arcaid/John Edward Linden/Architect: Richard Meier